How to manage for
tomorrow

How to manage for tomorrow

EUGENE J. BENGE

1975

DOW JONES-IRWIN, INC.
Homewood, Illinois 60430

First Printing, January 1975

Library of Congress Cataloging in Publication Data
Benge, Eugene Jackson, 1896–
    How to manage for tomorrow.

    1. Industrial management—United States. I. Title.
HD70.U5B4 658.4   74–18118
ISBN 0-87094-088-0

Printed in the United States of America

Foreword

IN THIS IMPORTANT BOOK, Eugene Benge lifts a corner of the curtain covering the future. He allows the reader to take a peek at what, in his opinion, is ahead for managers and management.

At the same time the author understands that, as much fun as it might be to predict management in the year 2000, the best he can really do is project those of today's trends that are already discernible. New management practices and techniques will not necessarily mean discarding old ways. More likely, much that will be called "new" will be refinements or evolutionary changes in the old ways—or old, proven ways given new names.

That is not to say that management and managers will not change. But readers of this book will not be given the false notion that, because a supertanker today displaces 400,000 dwt compared to its 30,000 dwt predecessor of a generation ago, it is growth alone that has created management problems that call for solutions. Rather, the author tells us how companies evolve, specialize, organize, reorganize, and develop successful management practices that all companies can use, and should use, regardless of size. And the most important factor in developing management practices is people.

Perhaps this book's most important contribution comes when the author turns to the changing attitudes of workers —blue- and white-collar alike. He states, unequivocally, that since people have changed, work must. Since it is a function of management to delineate work and help workers achieve (whether by participatory means or not), Benge shows us some pitfalls of failure to change work. He points to new approaches in managing that are needed—and ones that will happen, no matter how resistant to change some managers may be.

The author has divided this book into five parts: Coming Events Cast Their Shadows; People Will Still Be the Most Important Factor; A New Look at Business Functions; Tomorrow's Environment; and Tomorrow's Managers. It is interesting, as well as instructive, to note how much information on how business operates is packed into Part Three, A New Look at Business Functions. Almost in a nutshell, Benge covers the essentials of production, sales, marketing, and control. Many volumes, or entire series, have been written about each of these functions. Yet here, in one short section, is enough information to give you an important review of what it takes to make a business go.

The theme of the final part of this book, Tomorrow's Manager, is set by the words *know, do,* and *be.* It will no longer be enough for a manager to do things right. To do things right might be efficient. But, to be effective (and it is vital to our very system that future managers be effective) managers must, as consultant Peter Drucker tells us, have the ability to get the right things done. Few things will be more important to you, the reader, than to learn what you must *be* (as well as what you must *know* and *do*). For it is upon the rock of what you should be that you can build your own foundation for developing your ability to get the right things done.

While the author professes to have no magic formula or secret elixir for instant success, he does insist that what you will *be,* your very being, depends upon your character, temperament, abilities, and interests. These are the foundations of success. As the author develops his thoughts on each of these four factors, it becomes increasingly apparent that as important as what you should know and do are, what you should *be* is the essential ingredient needed to qualify for a high managerial post.

This is not a pretentious book. It is a practical one. For it interweaves social impact questions with economic ones. It challenges a growing belief that only government can do things right. It exhorts business to tell its story. It is unafraid to discuss the new attitudes of the young. Most of all it provides any manager, or prospective manager, with a channel buoy that will help him, or her, steer the way through the contrary currents of the decade of management ahead.

December 1974   JAMES M. JENKS, President
                    Alexander Hamilton Institute

Preface

THIS BOOK describes those changes and opportunities which seem to lie ahead in the field of management.

Opportunity, according to the humorist, is meeting the wolf at the door—and coming out the next day in a fur coat. By analogy, management opportunity is meeting the challenge of change and coming up with an important managerial job.

Since 1950, the McGraw-Hill Publications Company has issued forecasts on *The American Economy*. Typically these forecasts peer into the crystal ball for a long look ahead. Thus, the economists who have prepared the McGraw-Hill material believe that 1985 will see:

> *Total national output*—about $1.73 trillion of goods and services (77% more than in 1970).
>
> *Population*—240 million, up 17.3% from 1970.
>
> *Employment*—over 100 million, up 22 million over 1970.
>
> *Business capital expenditures*—$144 billion, compared with about $80 billion in 1970.
>
> *Consumer expenditures*—over $1.1 trillion, compared with about $616 billion in 1970.[1]

---

[1] Quoted by permission of the McGraw-Hill Publications Company, N.Y.

No one can doubt the impact of these startling figures on management practices. Opportunities, too!

Fifty years ago, managers in business were mainly concerned with productivity and distribution. Currently, added responsibilities are being thrust upon them by social pressures or legislation. Management and government must join hands to attack social problems, using the know-how and techniques of both social and physical sciences. Yet there exists an appalling shortage of men and women trained in *both* scientific areas.

The dawning socioindustrial complex will demand new viewpoints of industrial and governmental managers. They must attempt to forecast the future, must set goals and establish priorities. It's a global problem—we live in a shrinking world.

In all sciences, much more is known than is practiced. Years elapse from discovery to application. The author hopes to shorten this gap by bringing to the attention of managers and those who want to become managers, the things they should KNOW and DO and BE to meet the onrushing future.

December 1974   EUGENE J. BENGE

Acknowledgments

A NUMBER of friends and authorities have contributed generously to this book. My grateful appreciation goes to:

Lawrence A. Appley	Chairman of the Board, American Management Associations
Guy B. Arthur	President, Guy Arthur & Associates, Inc.
Richard N. Arthur	Senior V.P., Donnelly Mirrors, Inc.
Harold G. Brown, Jr.	Division Manager, DuPont
Samuel L. H. Burk	Personnel Consultant
Mark B. Cohen	Management Planning, Bowery Savings Bank
William J. Crockett	V.P. Human Relations, Saga Administrative Corporation
E. Mandell de Windt	Chairman of the Board, Eaton Corporation
R. W. Feagles	Senior V.P., First National City Bank
Joseph Ferreira	Manager, Diebold Research Group
James O. Hayes	President, American Management Assns.
Carl Heyel	Management Counsel
Donald O. Imsland	Consultant, Northern States Power Co.
James M. Jenks	President, Alexander Hamilton Institute
John Kane	Manager, Press Relations, Hewlett Packard Co.

Paul W. Kayser	Ex. V.P., Golightly and Company
William Latham	Executive Director, Society for Advancement of Management
Arnold F. McKenney	Training Coordinator, Riegel Products Corp.
Donald B. Miller	Past President, Society for Advancement of Management
J. W. Miller, Jr.	V.P. Personnel and Organization for a large corporation
Dr. Charles A. Myers	Director, Industrial Relations Section MIT
William C. Patterson	Principal, Wm. E. Hill and Co., Inc.
Walter J. Pedicord	V.P. Personnel, IBM
Charles H. Percy	U.S. Senator, Illinois
Kenneth A. Propp	Laboratory Administrator, IBM
Robin Roark	Partner, Hay Associates
Al Seares	Retired V.P., Remington Rand
Harold F. Smiddy	Retired V.P., General Electric Co.
J. N. Smith, Jr.	Consultant, Alcan Western Products
William D. Stevens	Professor, Dept. of Marketing, University of Florida
Edward A. Tomeski	Professor of Management, Fordham University
M. C. Turbyfill	V.P., Hickory Furniture Company
Malcolm W. Warren	Director, Management Development, Questor Corporation
Dr. Dale Yoder	Director, Bureau of Business Research, California State University
Lewis W. Zeyher	President, Zeyher Associates

In addition to the above list, there were a few others who because of modesty or for other reasons, asked that their names be omitted.

E. J. B.

Contents

part three
The new look of business functions

part four
Tomorrow's environment

part one

Coming events cast their shadows

1

The old order changeth—and a new order cometh!

IF CHANGE is the essence of progress, then the United States in general and management in particular are both on the verge of a tremendous leap forward into that awesome void we call the Future.

Up to the time of the Industrial Revolution, man's quest for a better life had inched ahead with faltering steps. The Stone Age merged into the Bronze Age and the Bronze Age into the Iron Age. Man rounded the sledge into a wheel and learned to harness waterpower and wind. In agriculture the water buffalo, the ox, and the horse supplemented man's muscles. Woven cloth gradually replaced skins for keeping man warm. He moved from a gloomy cave to a sunlit house built of stones, brick, or wood.

The Industrial Revolution, born in the middle of the 18th century, transferred production from the peasant's cottage to an entrepreneur's factory. From then to the present day, invention after invention have provided means of productivity heretofore unknown. Transportation and communication have made giant strides.

The factory system of production necessitated management. It was an autocratic management, usually provided by the entrepreneur-owner. His word was law. He made the

3

4

decisions and was successful to the extent that his decisions were sound or were adjusted to the time. Authoritarian management survives to this day, although social pressures are forcing fundamental changes in it.

About the turn of the present century, a new movement known as scientific management surfaced, spearheaded by the work of Frederick W. Taylor. It coincided with, and accelerated the transition from, an agricultural to an industrial society. In essence Taylor and his disciples advocated the substitution of science and measurement for trial and error or for judgment based on mere experience. He believed that the interests of owners and employees were identical, so that maximum output would benefit both. He advanced an idea that is only currently coming to be accepted; namely, that if each employee is developed to his greatest capacity, he will make the greatest contribution to prosperity. The term scientific management was not applied to the new philosophy and procedures until 1910.

Scientific management

Scientific management offered a new way of thinking about the whole problem of management. It introduced a number of techniques and devices that came to be more readily accepted than the basic philosophy itself. Some of these devices were:

1. Setting of work standards by time study (and later by motion study);
2. Payment of a bonus for achieving "standard time";
3. Fractionation of factory supervision into specialized foremen jobs to handle parts of the total task;
4. Standardization of methods, tools, and parts;
5. Planning and scheduling of work;
6. Standard practice instructions;
7. Production costing; and
8. The use of production control methods.

Despite opposition of organized labor and many managers, the new methods received growing acceptance. Productivity, profits, capital, and employee earnings increased rapidly. America became the wealthiest nation in the world.

The foundation of the free enterprise system is capital, which provides workers with machinery, equipment, and materials. By supplementing human effort with energy-driven equipment, high productivity is achieved.

Even Karl Marx, German philosopher and founder of world communism, begrudgingly wrote, "Capitalism has been the first to show what man's activity can bring about. It has accomplished wonders, far surpassing Egyptian pyramids, Roman aqueducts, and Gothic cathedrals. During its rule of scarce 100 years, it has created more massive and more colossal productive forces than have all preceding generations together." One wonders why, after such an encomium, Marx advocated the downfall of capitalism!

Wars accelerate technology

World War I, 1914 to 1918, injected new dynamism and new thinking into the productive capacity of our nation. The war put great accent on production and hence on production technology. Labor shortages brought about greater interest in employee relations problems.

Military science, well advanced as to problems of organization, became known to managers; many of its concepts were adopted, such as chain of command, span of control, line and staff relationships, and organization charts.

Other nations were similarly affected, especially those at war. There were scarcities of raw materials as well as of labor. Companies poorly set up to handle war orders suddenly found themselves with volumes of orders far beyond their wildest dreams. As always in wartime, prices rose sharply. In such a situation it was inevitable that managements should effect great change in their attitudes toward customers, employees, the government, and methods of production. Another effect of the first World War was that management became conscious of itself as a class, and the term "management profession" came into use. In this book we shall detail the changes in management philosophy, practices and organization relationships that have occurred over the present century, using this material as background for a projection of things to come.

Management is not a thing apart from our social structure but is actually one of society's most valuable resources. It finds itself involved in many of the problems of society, such as urban redevelopment, poverty, crime, minorities, environment, fuel shortages, housing, medical care, education, and inflation. Social planners advocate a coordinated business–government attack on many of these problems, probably to work in conjunction with universities and various social research agencies.

More and more managers are coming to grips with the high rate of social change, which frequently imposes additional burdens on their jobs, sometimes confuses them, and often diverts their time and energies from the affairs of the businesses they control. A few companies have come to believe that such diverted energy is well spent.

The Northern States Power Company, for example, faced with opposition from environmentalists, took a number of significant steps. It:

1. Invited representatives from the Minnesota state government, and from selected citizens' groups to participate in new plant site selection and in modifications of marketing policy;

2. Established a "Future Trends" training program for higher level managers;

3. Developed a second training program, called "Futures Reports," a series of eight 90-minute sessions, for other personnel.

Donald O. Imsland, the consultant who conceived this forward-looking plan, tells me that the company is prepared to make the program available to other companies and civic groups—an outstanding example of corporate responsibility.

A long look ahead

The Hudson Institute is a non-profit research center for the study of major problems affecting our country. One of its most important publications, *The Year 2000*, forecasts what our world will probably be like a generation hence.

The Institute foresees a U.S. growth rate annually of 3 percent; a per capita gross national product of more than

$10,000; a continuing decrease in the work week; more leisure activities; an increasing economic gap between the have and have-not nations; a world population that will approach six billion; a U.S. *labor* force of 139 million people; average hourly earnings in manufacturing of $11.50; business investment in new plant double that of 1975; family income to double that of 1975; affluence, causing a collapse of the work ethic; accents on intangibles that money cannot buy; growing indifference to financial success; a fairly high poverty "floor"; deviations from social conformity; continued youth rebellion against "obsolete" values; governmental paternalism; decline of traditional religions.

Despite trends toward greater freedom of the individual, middle class people will continue to be work- and achievement-oriented. They will emphasize self-improvement, culture, suburban living, travel and self-indulgence. The very wealthy will continue to exercise pervasive social power.

The future offers challenging opportunity for managers to improve the productivity of service occupations—including teachers, doctors, lawyers, and social workers. Hospitals, government institutions, food distribution, maintenance and repair services, to cite a few, have not kept pace with the productivity of manufacturing, commerce, and public utilities.

The Industrial Revolution, buttressed by scientific management has so far met man's material needs in the advanced countries. Affluence is now diverting men's energies and interest away from material satisfactions toward emotional satisfactions: in work itself, or from products, pleasing packaging, and numerous services. Many far-seeing researchers are speculating as to the future role of the manager in such a changed economic milieu. They see him as dispensing services with great sensory or psychological appeals, frequently as "sugar coating" for orthodox products or leisure activities. Most managers dislike this unflattering preview of their future role.

In the future, it will be easier to loaf through life than in the past. For those who want achievement and material advancement, there will likely be less competition and hence more opportunity to get ahead.

Maybe not all these predicted changes will occur in the near future, but if only half of them do so, the effect on management will obviously be significant. In all advanced nations of the world, products and services must meet future needs and therefore will be planned, executed, and controlled by managers of one kind or another.

A disquieting factor will be shortages of the Earth's raw materials. History will likely record that when the smooth-flowing stream of affluence encountered the shoals of scarcity, great turbulence ensued.

Social change is accelerating and hence changes in management to adapt to society must likewise accelerate. The inflexible attitudes of past managers are unsuited to present problems and to future management approaches.

Education

An important trend for the near future deals with education of young people.

The period immediately following World War II was one of high birth rates; that era seems to be over. American couples are marrying later and producing fewer children. As a consequence the proportion of young people of high school age is expected to decrease in the years ahead. Somewhat the same should happen to the college age group. However, both black and white youths are better educated than before, and this statement is especially true for blacks. Something like 80% of young adults in the age group 25 to 29 are currently high school graduates and almost 20% are college graduates. Since this is the age group from which managers are normally recruited, the outlook is good even though the supply may be diminishing. Americans are becoming better educated with each generation.

Alvin Toffler, author of the best seller *Future Shock,* served as editor of *Learning for Tomorrow,* to which 18 psychologists, social scientists, educators, and others contributed. The thesis of this thought-provoking book is that current education is oriented to the past and present, rather than to a new and vastly different future. The publishers term the work "a manifesto for the next wave of change in our educational institutions." A 50 page appendix suggests futurist studies that might well be included at various educational levels.

A socio-industrial complex

The coming socio-industrial complex will demand new viewpoints of both industrial and governmental managers. It will probably be necessary to set priorities, for many of the problems will be antithetical; *e.g.,* the aims of environmentalists are opposed to the aims of those who would provide more power. As suggested above, education will have to be more forward looking; instead of training for the past, it will need to train for the future. Past generations have made this same statement, but the need is now so great that educational leaders will finally have to take heed. There is and will be shortages of managerial talent, trained in both physical and social sciences. Some of this shortage may be alleviated by man's latest machine, the computer, which is rapidly changing our life style.

Aside from family management through inheritance, most managers have evolved through a process of the survival of the fittest. They are managers because they have learned how to manage better than their competitors. This statement is partially true in government service as well. Without doubt, the leadership of social change must fall on the shoulders of such men and women.

Social problems are not insulated islands; they relate one to another and often one causes another. Consider, for example, the relationships among production, education, minorities, opportunities, housing, and urban development. To attack any one alone has proven futile; a coordinated attack, using interdiscipline knowhow, can be an important contribution of managers to the future. Breakthroughs in production technology can augment social advancement and ease the tasks of those who are attempting to solve social problems. Consider the automobile, for example:

My grandfather owned a carriage not greatly different in structure or speed from Ben Hur's chariot. Then came the automobile. Around 1900 a few automobiles had been built in Europe and the United States. The speed limit in many communities was 12 miles per hour. One community was so fearful of the awesome new contraption that it passed a law that read as follows: "The speed limit on country roads this year will be a secret and the penalty for violation will be $10.00 for every mile an offender is caught going in excess of it." Until recently the automobile speed limit on many highways was 60 or 65 miles per hour.

Airplanes can travel ten or more times as fast as the automobile. Our generation has witnessed the emergence of space ships that travel at unbelievable speeds. How fast will some future generation travel?

Technological breakthroughs are not only a benefit to society at large. They contribute to business profits and cause alterations in management practices and organization structures. Some of these will be considered in this book.

Newspapers and other media are pointing out the great changes in attitude toward work of the present generation. Managers have long since noted some of these manifestations in indifference to work, quality, absenteeism, insubordination, labor turnover, and other out-croppings. We shall consider these new developments at some length in this book.

The whole field of industrial relations has burgeoned in recent decades. Selection, training, compensation, fringe benefits, union relationships and labor legislation have all caused great modifications in management practice.

Management itself has reacted to some of the problems and pressures upon it by placing great stress on results, rather than merely on activities. This is a relatively new accent in management, one that will be examined here.

Psychologists tell us that fundamental to human and animal intelligence is adaptation. In the past managers have shown remarkable powers of adaptation to change and there is no reason to believe that they will not continue to do so in the future.

The labor union movement too is experiencing the winds

of change. Union members are resenting the autocratic ways of some labor union leaders, are flouting their authority, or are refusing to uphold the agreements they have negotiated. In a later chapter we shall speculate on this trend and attempt to peer into the future as to the relationships of labor leaders and managers. Such speculation must also include the government, which in many respects has become something of a partner of the labor union movement.

New role for managers

Research findings of psychologists and sociologists are bringing into the picture some new thinking as to employer–employee relationships. Much of this thinking revolves around the concept of employee involvement in work, and will be explored in this book. The synergistic result of internal trends in management, combined with opportunities in the social environment, means that management in the future must be radically different than that which has existed to date.

In the past, managers have conformed to the organization's scheme of things. They had their places on an organization chart; they understood the lines of authority and were dubious as to how much authority they personally possessed. They had a vague idea as to the organization's goals and to the goals of their particular jobs. Rewards were outer-imposed, in contradistinction to internal feelings of worthwhileness.

Coming events will cast the new manager in a different mold. He will consider himself as a professional and will belong to professional societies in his particular area of competence. He will be mobile, ready to move to another employer if the new job promises greater independence or satisfaction of one sort or another. In making a sharp break with tradition, as he must do, he will find it a painful and stressful experience. New trends will not necessarily discard old ways; more likely they will add additional layers to the old. Many of the same conditions are occurring or will occur in most of the advanced industrialized nations of the world.

So interest yourself in the day after tomorrow.

Tomorrow's actions—NOW

You as a manager should study the forecasts of scientists who analyze and project significant social trends.

Seek out technological breakthroughs pertinent to your operations.

See the role of your company as part of a larger economic system for worldwide production and distribution of goods and services.

Great change is here; plan it rather than merely endure it.

If your company offers goods or services connected with housing or households, do long range planning under the assumption of standardized mass housing in communities that will coalesce into megalopolises.

If you are in a *service* industry, apply production management techniques to your company's activities.

If your product is tangible, research new supply sources and new raw materials.

Orient your thinking to a socio-governmental-industrial economy.

2

The big get bigger

growth—pro and con

LET US first accept that growth is an important objective, primarily because it normally can decrease cost per unit. If administrative expense, selling expense and fixed charges can be spread over a larger number of units produced or sold, the unit cost will decrease.

> I had an example of this in reverse very early in my business career. At that time I was working for a large oil refinery, which had a barrel plant. In this plant men repaired wooden barrels by hand. During a business recession, the plant manager ordered the superintendent of the barrel factory to lay off half the working force, which was done. Immediately the cost per barrel rose and I was assigned to investigate the reasons. It soon became apparent that although the total direct labor costs had been cut sharply, the allocation of salaries for the superintendent, a foreman, and a clerk were causing the additional cost per barrel.

Size enjoys other benefits. A large company can organize its own research staff for developing new products. It can set up a personnel department to improve selection and training. If it becomes big enough, it can have its own computer, which can confer benefits in many directions. Various kinds of standardization in production can often be developed.

13

Long range planning has contributed to corporate growth. The Stanford Research Institute, based on its study of why companies grow, reported that "those that now support planning programs have shown a superior growth rate in recent years."

Companies with over $50 million in annual sales make greater use of advanced management practices than smaller companies. Some of these practices are computer processing, management by objectives, organization development, job enrichment, and operations research. Whereas many activities of corporations have been decentralized, growth to large size has frequently caused *re*-centralization of management practices such as those listed above.

The descriptive adjective "big" has to be redefined in each successive generation. The word "supertanker" was used in the '40s to designate a ship that carried 28,000 tons of petroleum; current tankers carry 20 times as much. Some industrial equipment can produce ten times the output of ten years earlier, resulting in "economies of scale." Reliability and quality usually are improved also.

Newer production equipment integrates many manufacturing processes, typically under control of a computer. Handling of parts is eliminated, inventory control is tightened, machine precision approaches "zero defects." Numerical control of machine tools, presses, or injection molding offers considerable flexibility in size and shape of parts produced.

There are limitations on size, however:
1. Availability and cost of money for large investments;
2. Markets to absorb a continuous output of standardized units; costs of idle equipment;
3. Operating skills required;
4. Maintenance;
5. Obsolescence;
6. Companies that have been awarded a large government contract operate under some new constraints, imposed by Big Brother as a virtual partner. Aside from contractual obligations, companies have to follow hiring and other legislative requirements and face possible renegotiation at the termination of the contract.

Some socio-economists foresee the rise of a "contract state" in the near future, a crossbreeding of private enterprise and a corporate state that will reveal some aspects of fascism.

There can be other detriments to size. Contacts with, and service to, customers may lessen. On large orders, customers may demand such heavy discounts that the profit disappears. Manufacturing to a customer's specifications becomes more difficult, and flexibility in relationships with many customers disappears. Despite these possible disadvantages, most companies opt for growth.

Writing in "Management—Tasks, Responsibilities, Practices,"[1] Peter Drucker says, "Very big companies should test themselves to find the point beyond which further size . . . produces dis-economies" and "think through how to give birth to new independent businesses that then have the capacity for growth . . ." "There is a point of complexity beyond which a business is no longer manageable."

One result of bigness has been vulnerability to lawsuits filed in Federal District Courts. These have more than doubled in a ten year period, and the trend continues.

Suits relating to patents, copyrights, and trademarks have decreased from 33 to 21 percent of the total. Antitrust suits have trebled in number and have increased in the percentage of the total, from 9 to 13. Securities regulations' suits have multiplied *seven times* in number and the percentage of the total has trebled from 6 to 18. Cases involving labor law—principally union disputes with employers—represent almost half the problem, and cases of this kind have doubled over the last decade.

Other lawsuits pertain to environment and fair employment practices.

It is evident that managers in the future must have a working knowledge of legislation dealing with antitrust, securities, patents, copyright and trademarks, labor relations, and environment. This situation will often involve supervising "in-house" legal staffs.

---

[1] Published by Harper and Row, N.Y., 1974.

Public fear of size

People in general and the government in particular have been distrustful of large companies. Witness the Sherman Antitrust Law, which was passed as far back as 1890. In 1911 the huge Standard Oil Trust was broken up by a Supreme Court decision.

Successful small companies live in constant fear of the voracious maw of industrial behemoths. Purchases of large blocs of stock, stock "raiding," small company dependence on huge orders from a large corporation, and full-page ads of attractive offers to stockholders have characterized many enforced takeovers.

In the popular mind, fear of bigness revolves around possible monopoly; *i.e.*, sufficient control over markets to enable a company to price its products with little regard for the forces of competition. Unfortunately, trust busters of the government have come to attack, not monopoly, but bigness itself, without trying to distinguish between the two. Laws and court decisions have endeavored to prevent combinations in restraint of trade, price fixing, stock manipulation, and other actions inimical to the public good.

Foreign nations have not followed this same thinking, in fact they have often fostered bigness. The cartels of Europe actually divide up markets and encourage bigness. Japan, with an eye toward growth through world trade, has encouraged mergers in its steel industry, its banks, its petrochemical industry, its shipping firms, and others. Growth there has not been accomplished by "takeovers" as in the United States but rather has been fostered by goverment sanction. As an example, the Mistsubishi Bank, with deposits of over ten billion dollars, is the central financing core of a group that includes about 50 companies with interlocking stockholdings whose total sales run about 26 billion dollars—more than ten percent of the nation's gross national product. It is the viewpoint of the Japanese government that such size must be encouraged to compete in international markets. Not many American and European companies have sales greater than Mistsubishi.

The ten largest corporations in the United States are in order of size General Motors, Exxon, Ford, General Electric, Chrysler, International Business Machines, Mobil Oil, Texaco, Western Electric, and International Telephone and Telegraph. Taken as a group the sales of these ten large companies would be well over 100 billion dollars. As an example of the widespread influence of a single corporation, consider that ITT owns or controls Sheraton Hotels, Avis cars, Morton Frozen Foods, Who's Who in America, Bobbs-Merrill Publishing Company, and 400 others around the world!

If the trend toward big corporations continues, which seems likely, some economists believe that within a decade or two, 300 large corporations may largely determine the economy of the world and even dominate the national governments that try to control them.

Mergers

The term merger is used to include a number of different types. It is also used synonymously with the words acquisition, consolidation, or amalgamation. Mergers stem from the visions of high level executives who have been bitten by the bug of entrepreneurial giantism.

In the history of our country, mergers seem to have run in waves with an interval of 30 or 40 years between the peaks. The first one occurred in 1899 when over 1,200 were recorded. This was the period when U.S. Steel and International Harvester came into being. Three years later the number of mergers was recorded as fewer than 400; ten years later fewer than 100.

The second peak occurred in 1929 when again more than 1,200 mergers were recorded. This particular period saw the birth of RCA, Caterpillar Tractor, and Chrysler.

The year 1968 saw a third peak, this time revealing about 2,400 mergers of manufacturing and mining companies.

No one can say that there will be another 30 or 40 year interval before the next peak arises. There have been specific contributing factors to each of these three peaks, but factors that were different each time. To understand these differences, it is necessary to consider the various types of mergers that are possible.

In the horizontal merger, two or more companies engaged in the production or sale of much the same products are combined. This was the predominant type around the turn of the century. For example, 170 companies were welded into the U.S. Steel Corporation. The result of various horizontal mergers was a high concentration in industries like steel, farm machinery, copper, chemicals, and cans.

A vertical merger can reach back to sources of raw materials, or forward to conversion of products into retail items. Thus a paper manufacturer might acquire a pulp mill and a paper bag plant. The merger wave of the 1920s included both horizontal and vertical types and increased corporate concentration in our economy. This second surge of mergers ended with the 1929 stock market crash.

The gigantic third wave saw the birth of conglomerates, with top financial officers playing the role of obstetrician. It brought together firms whose products were not related, either horizontally or vertically. It was characterized by combining companies from varied industries, requiring different production techniques or different marketing channels. Sometimes the motivating factor was new uses for raw materials (such as wood pulp) or different applications of production technology (such as electronics). As a consequence of the third merger wave, which began in the 1950s and reached its peak about 1968 or 1969, the 200 largest manufacturing companies controlled nearly two-thirds of the assets of all U.S. manufacturing corporations.

The reasons given by companies for reaching out to acquire other companies are many and varied. As shown below, they can be classified under five major headings: market position, public image, manufacturing, finance, and management. There can of course be others.

1. To improve market position
    a. Product diversification; replace product obsolescence
    b. Get new customers; widen markets
    c. Supplement seasonal products

    d. Increase sales volume and percentage of sales expense
    e. Meet or reduce competition

2. To improve public image
    a. Prestige of owner or management
    b. Power in community or politics

3. To improve manufacturing
    a. Acquire a new process, or a new raw material
    b. Reduce costs
    c. Eliminate duplicate production facilities
    d. Larger research and development effort

4. To improve the financial position
    a. Wider credit from banks or suppliers
    b. Tax losses
    c. Price/earnings ratio of stock
    d. Profits through exchange of stock

5. To improve management competence
    a. Administrative skill
    b. Technical knowledge
    c. Competent workforce
    d. Avoid punitive state legislation

    One instance which came to my attention was that of a relatively uneducated president of a successful company who wanted to buy a company for a personal reason. It seemed that the second company had been instrumental in organizing a country club in a very select community. The president of the acquiring company was willing to invest the funds of his company so that he and his wife would be able to move in a higher level social circle. The ultimate effect was that he was accepted in the country club but not in the homes of the families he was trying to crack.

This true story suggests that a company contemplating an acquisition should prepare guidelines for acquisitions such as the following:

1. A proposed acquisition should fit into the acquiring company's long range plan;
2. The two companies should (usually) be integrated into one organization, with similar policies, procedures, and standards;
3. Good communications are needed;
4. Unprofitable assets or products should normally be disposed of;
5. By joint agreement, responsibilities and authorities should be reduced to writing; standards of performance set; methods of control (accountability) established;
6. Poor performing managers should be replaced;
7. Flexibility and adaptability to change are needed;
8. Broad-gauge managers must be developed;
9. Net earnings should increase more than sales;
10. Return on investment should increase.

Some mergers prove unprofitable

Not all mergers and certainly not all conglomerate mergers have lived up to expectations. In fact some of the overly ambitious conglomerate mergers have been disastrous. The Federal Trade Commission made a study of nine huge conglomerates and came to a number of conclusions:

1. In the period 1960 to 1968, these nine companies had acquired 340 companies with ten billion dollars of assets;
2. The conglomerates made only minor changes in the operation of the firms they had acquired;
3. The study found no evidence that gathering together a large number of disparate companies increased efficiency;
4. The mergers did little if anything to reduce competition in their respective industries. They were scattered in such varied industries that they did not corral such market power that they could control prices.
5. The published financial reports, for the most part, were so generalized that a financial analyst could

scarcely determine what was happening in the respective units acquired. This last finding caused the authors of the report to recommend that highly diversified firms should be required by the government to provide sales and profit data for their various subsidiaries.

This study bears out Peter Drucker's contention that some organizations can balloon to such size that they are "no longer manageable." But this conclusion may hold true for the sophistication of the present generation of managers. If corporations continue to increase in size, as predicted, the future presents immense opportunities for those who steep themselves in management conceptual thinking needed to run giant corporations, conglomerates, and multi-nationals. Oliver Wendell Holmes one-time associate justice of the U.S. Supreme Court, in one of his famous decisions, wrote, "The reward of the general is not a bigger tent, but a larger command."

Why small companies survive

Despite all the purported advantages of big companies, you may be one of those individuals who wants to be free of the internal politics, impersonality, and ruthlessness of big corporations. If so you may either start your own business or seek employment with some small company.

Success of a small company requires a number of contributing factors, such as:

1. A product or an idea that is needed;
2. Adequate investment and working capital;
3. The proper know-how to produce the product or service;
4. Marketing ability;
5. Good accounting records;
6. Proper management;
7. Research for new products, methods, materials, equipment, money sources, markets, significant legislation, and economic trends;
8. Long hours and determination.

The Small Business Administration, an independent federal government agency, operates through ten regional offices, 53 district offices and several dozen other locations. It is designed to "aid, counsel, assist, and protect the interests of small business concerns." The SBA provides a number of services, and if you are in a small business for yourself, or associated with a small business firm, you are well advised to get in touch with the nearest SBA office to learn more about these services.

The harsh facts are that only about 15 percent of small businesses survive for one year, and that the number of self-employed persons is decreasing. For those that do survive, the U.S. Department of Commerce offers additional services through publications and other assistance from the Office of Business Economics, the Bureau of the Census, the Bureau of Domestic Commerce, the Bureau of International Commerce, the Economic Development Administration, the Office of Minority Business Enterprise, the National Technical Information Service, the Patent Office, and the Maritime Administration. For the small businessman determined to succeed, Uncle Sam offers a lot of assistance.

Some small companies reach the point where they can no longer make progress and should consider being taken over by a larger organization.

A friend provides a case in point. He and his brother operate a small concern that provides auto supplies to a list of loyal customers. For years they were successful, operating their own warehouse with a staff of six people. In recent years a number of pressures are pushing them to the wall. Chain stores are underselling them. Rent for their warehouse has increased. Labor turnover has given them personnel problems. Located in a high-crime neighborhood, they have had to hire a night watchman. Suppliers have been bought out by large companies. This little organization is now reduced to the point that my friend and his brother do everything without any help. About all they have left to offer customers is quick service, which, however, is frequently delivered at no profit or at personal expenditure of time and energy. The time has come for these two partners to accept one of several offers to buy them out, but pride interferes and they struggle on.

Here are some reasons why a small business should consider being acquired by a larger unit:

1. Personal reasons—health, desire to retire, preference for liquidity, absence of a manager successor;
2. Marketing. Loss of market position resulting from competition, obsolescence of product, expiration of patent protection, termination of contract, market saturation, changing market demands;
3. Investment—insufficient return on capital, opportunity for investment elsewhere, shrinking profit margins;
4. Outlook—conflicts among present owners, new competing companies, puzzling changes in technology, need for costly research and development, and changing economic conditions;
5. Offer of a good job with the acquiring company.

One solution that has been adopted by successful small companies is to "go public." This means to incorporate and sell shares to the general public. Normally this step is undertaken when additional capital is needed or when the original investors seek to translate assets into ready cash. Going public offers many pitfalls, including high underwriting costs, risks of raiding by investors who may take control of the company, possible illegalities, or unsuccessful stock issuance. Competent advice is needed at all stages.

In years gone by, lack of sufficient capital was a prime reason for failure of new companies. In recent years, bankruptcy of both new and established companies has resulted more from managerial incompetence, principally lack of managerial experience; failure to coordinate all activities; inadequate sales; superior competition; credit and collections; and fraud.

The U.S. Bureau of Labor reports that since 1962 the number of self-employed persons, nine million at that time, has fallen at the rate of about 200,000 per year. Self-employment is precarious, albeit personally rewarding.

In the years ahead, more and more companies will set up a single control center. It will reveal charts, and data pertaining to budgets, costs, production, quality, markets, long-range plans, employee relations, social accountabilities, etc. In small companies, the control center may be a binder on the president's desk. In very large companies it may be an entire room that will also contain facilities for querying various computers stationed throughout the organization.

In summary you need to understand the forces that have contributed and continue to contribute to bigness in many of society's institutions—industry, commerce, finance, and government. You need further to understand the managerial problems that attend bigness in these institutions. Even if you contemplate business for yourself or working for a small company, it is still desirable to understand the successful management practices of big companies.

Tomorrow's actions—NOW

Apply decision-making techniques before your company diversifies products or enters new industries.

Evaluate whether planned growth in volume will yield greater profits per dollar invested—or merely more problems.

Cultivate additional sources of increasingly scarce capital.

From observation, reading and study, list additional management practices that might be of benefit to your company.

If your company is publicly owned, prepare in advance a strategy against an enforced takeover by some large corporation or group of investors.

List the guidelines, as well as the advantages and disadvantages, for your company to acquire others.

List your company's limitations on growth, including legal and governmental constraints. Optimum size may be more important than maximum.

If you own or manage a small company, list the reasons why you can compete with large companies. Additionally, list the pros and cons of being acquired by a larger organization.

Initiate and maintain long range planning, including corporate *profit* planning.

Spell out how your company will fit into a future world dotted with mammoth centers for collecting raw materials to be transported to central processing areas; also multi-warehouse centers from which tributary distribution will emanate.

3

Who's in charge
around here?

Evolution of a company

MOST companies start small, and if successful, grow along
lines of the pyramidal organization. When the company is
small, not much attention is paid to sharp lines of demarcation among jobs. The owner-manager will perform almost
any activity required, as will the first few employees he hires.
Gradually specialization takes place. Some one individual
takes care of procurement; one or more handle production;
some one does record-keeping; one or more oversee sales
and delivery.

The first stage of growth largely represents merely adding
people as needed in these respective functions.

Ten or twenty years later the company has been successful. By now the various functions are clearly defined.
Moreover, some staff jobs have come into being—planning and scheduling of production; quality control; advertising and sales promotion; cost accounting; office tasks for
billing, collections, accounts payable, and other record
keeping functions. Stratification has occurred—there are
employees, group leaders, foremen, a plant manager, perhaps a vice president, a treasurer or comptroller, and the

25

president of the company. The organization chart shows a typical pyramidal structure, with staff jobs appended at various levels.

With continued growth, the company may decentralize by setting up a counterpart plant in some other region of the country; or it may turn over the production of some one product to a plant devoted solely to the manufacture of that product. Similarly in the marketing function, branch sales offices may be set up, or specialized sales activities developed for particular products.

Whereas the original organization developed along functional lines, the decentralization may be either divisionalization by geography or divisionalization by product. These developments may not alter the basic pyramidal chart but they may make it more complex, so that it comes to look like innocuous doodling rather than planned structuring.

Characteristic of the functional organization is that managers of the principal functions report directly to the president or, later, to an executive vice president.

In the typical geographic divisionalization, considerable autonomy is delegated to the plant manager, or to the division sales manager. Sometimes a subsidiary company is organized, with its own president and board of directors, many of whom will interlock with the directors of the parent company. Combinations of production and marketing are possible. Thus, one plant may supply many division sales offices; conversely, one sales organization may sell for the products of a number of plants.

In product divisionalization, one plant is assigned to produce one family of products and/or a specialized sales force sells only one class of products.

Figure 1, "Three Types of Organization," contrasts functional, geographic divisional and product divisional structures.

Policies and practices that may be successful with a strictly functional organization may have to be altered for either a geographic divisional or product divisional organization. Careful study needs to be given to staff activities necessary for such decentralization. Usually pertinent staff people re-

Figure 1
THREE TYPES OF ORGANIZATION

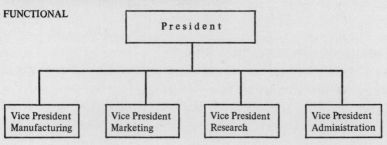

FUNCTIONAL

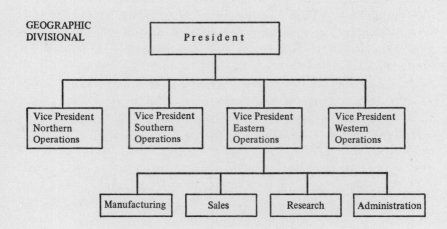

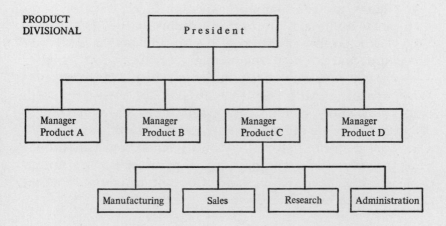

port to the head of a local unit but have an indirect, technical relationship with corporate staff personnel at the home office.

Signs that point to reorganization

It is important that top management recognize the signs that suggest restructuring the organization. Some of these signs are:

1. Conflict between high level line and high level staff executives, or among high level line executives or between corporate and division staff people.
2. A number of executives have "assistants" and "assistants to." This condition may indicate a failure to delegate. Secretaries, assistants and "assistants to" are typically assigned to people and not to work. They usually "think like the boss" and derive their importance and salary status from the importance and salary status of the principal. There is an implicit derogation in this situation. Some companies have abolished the title "assistant to" in the entire organization.
3. Radical changes of policies or procedures when the impact of new ideas rolls over stupidity or stagnation. Such changes may require alteration in reporting lines on the organization chart, particularly if too many key men have been directly responsible to any given top level executive.
4. There are too many organization levels between foreman and decision-making authority. If a decision is bounced from a foreman to assistant superintendent to superintendent to plant manager, or even to higher levels, you have a situation in which authority commensurate with responsibility has not been delegated.
5. Too many committees. Committees have usefulness in bringing out viewpoints or specialized knowledge, but majority votes of committee members (sometimes a wishy-washy compromise) can rarely be substituted for an executive decision. Committees should advise, but one executive decide.

6. Inadequate communication, especially lateral communication. If a foreman can get information from foremen in other departments only by going through their respective department heads, we have bureaucracy and probably empire building by high level executives.

7. Mergers almost invariably change the structure of an organization. Duplications must be eliminated, fears allayed, personnel evaluated, jealousies lessened, staffs combined, job descriptions rewritten, and the organization chart redrawn.

8. Product diversification can cause changes in the organization structure. New products may require their own methods of manufacture or of marketing. They may tax production facilities, so that a second shift may be indicated in a particular plant. They may replace some unprofitable product with the resulting personnel and systems changes.

9. Opportunity arises for setting up profit centers. The decentralized profit center is particularly applicable to geographic or product divisionalizations; in essence managers of these units are in business for themselves. Changes in accounting or budgetary practices are necessary. The allocation of general and administrative expense from the home office can either make or break the profit picture of a divisionalized plant or product. If a company has been highly centralized with one big boss, the chances are high that risk-taking managers equal to directing the operations of decentralized profit centers will not be available.

    For divisionalized, decentralized organizations, profit centers can be very useful—they are a form of control or accountability for such decentralizations. They are less indicated for highly centralized organizations of a functional type or for single product manufacturing.

10. Prolonged tolerance of ineptitude or obsolescence in a key executive requires high level decisiveness accompanied by humane handling: new title, new re-

sponsibilities, special research assignment, etc. Each such case is difficult—but must be handled for the larger good of the organization.

There are some factors at work that are bringing about *re*-centralization. True decentralization involves delegation of authority to the decentralized locations; if this authority is poorly exercised by the managers at those locations, top management will be disappointed with the results and will either increase the number of controls or will recentralize some of the activities which have previously been delegated. The electronic computer is another recentralizing force—top management feels that the computer can help it make important decisions much better than could divisionalized managers. Sophisticated operations research usually requires a computer for its implementation and since rather few individuals have the know-how to conduct such research, it will normally be centralized at the home office. Virtually all companies continue to centralize, in top management or in the board of directors, decisions as to large capital investments. Neither decentralization nor centralizations in management can be classed as good or bad; each situation calls for study to determine which practice is most likely to be effective in each situation.

Weaknesses of hierarchical organizations

There are three principal forms of hierarchical organization, owner managed, partnerships, and corporations.

In general, the first two reveal a somewhat unstructured functional organization, with a close relationship between top managers and workers and a continuing thrust for profit *maximization.*

The corporation, on the other hand, is usually rigidly structured, reveals a stratified "pecking order," suffers a considerable gap between top managers and workers, and aims for steady growth of profits in contradistinction to maximization.

Corporate ownership is normally distributed among many owners; the board of directors is satisfied with profit growth.

Top managers may become more interested in self-aggrandizement and in defending their entrenched positions than in stockholder interests.

> At one time in my career I was a director of a medium sized manufacturing company. A majority of the directors, who were also top executives in the company, spent many hours scheming how to feather their own nests, rather than how to increase profits for the owners. Finally I resigned in protest. As might be expected, the company's stock has steadily gone down hill.

Birds and animals defend the areas that supply them with food. Salesmen want exclusive territories. Foremen resent intrusions into their shops. Department heads insist on clear definitions of their responsibilities. Vice presidents build "empires." As a consequence, some corporations are agglomerations of staked-out domains rather than smoothly integrated parts of the whole.

Bureaucratic structure risks stagnation; *e.g.:*

1. Lower levels of managers tend to carry out only those portions of top level instructions that do not conflict with their concepts of self-interest. Alternately, they will avoid risk in decisions or pass the buck upward.

2. These same lower levels tend to prevent upward flow of negative information, or, if a cost or budget system "spills the beans," managers may alibi.

> The autocratic head of a huge manufacturer decided to distribute products through retail stores. Actually the move was unprofitable, but to the day of his death his immediate associates juggled acccounting records to show a profit for the retail end of the business.

3. "Red tape" becomes costly and slows up the ability of the organization to act in emergencies or react to change.

> A case in point was told me by the night operator of a machine in a metal working plant: "The reciprocating spring broke. It's a simple repair job; when I had my own shop, I'd replaced those springs a half dozen times. But here I had to fill out Form 230—Machine Repair Needed. I gave it to the night foreman. Since the parts department was locked, all he

could do was turn it over to his relief next morning, who inspected the machine, approved Form 230, and sent it to the maintenance foreman. He filled out a requisition; a maintenance mechanic got the spring. The machine was idle for nine hours; it took five minutes to fix it."

4. By far the greatest weakness of the pyramidal structure of most corporations is the gap from the lowest to the highest level. Many employees and foremen have never even seen the company president. "The management" is to them a nebulous but ominous group of powerful people who are paid undeserved fantastic salaries and bonuses, make impractical plans, and fail to understand the problems of people at lower levels.

Most managers in large companies have noted these and other weaknesses, but have felt powerless to do anything about them. Instead, they have accepted them as inescapable parts of the pyramidal organization structure. Organization development, discussed in a later chapter, attempts to overcome some of these weaknesses.

Since "the big get bigger," there is developing a need for highly trained organization analysts.

Companies that draw organization charts soon discover that the charts change rather quickly and then that they imperfectly present the actual relationships that exist among the members of an organization. Dotted lines inadequately depict secondary or indirect reporting relationships. Staff functions, such as the personnel department, have an almost direct relationship to many other departments. It becomes difficult to show the true interaction of divisionalized plants or sales offices to corporate staff departments. Usually such charts fail completely to take account of the hidden informal organization that exists in all companies.

A truly great executive welds together an articulated organization that can be operated by persons of lesser talents. He will cause charts to be drawn, and revised from time to time, so that the organizational skeleton at least will be understood by his subordinates. He is not disturbed by an inability to picture the entire gamut of inter-relationships on a single sheet of paper.

New organization concepts

Even where no alteration in the organization chart is indicated, certain changes are currently occurring in many companies. Rigid lines of authority are becoming more flexible, as authority is being diffused throughout the organization, most of it downward, but some of it laterally. This trend flattens the normal pyramidal structure by decreasing the number of levels between low and high jobs on the chart. Decision centers are moving closer to practical operations. Consultative relationships, occurring at various operational points, make unnecessary much vertical reporting or higher level decision making.

In line with the trend toward consultative relationships, consideration is being given to what is termed matrix management, illustrated in Figure 2. It has been in use for many years in large consulting engineering groups or in some research organizations. Typically it brings together specialized skills of a number of members of the organization for carrying out some project or contract. Prior to the organization of such an ad hoc group, sometimes called a task force, there must have been a detailed inventory of the knowledge and skills of the persons available. Sending a man to the Moon required a matrix organization, which called upon hundreds of specialists to accomplish such a tremendous result.

Detailed planning before undertaking a large project may well require preparation of a Critical Path Network or other chart, which in essence works backward from the expected results and deadline to establish who is to do what, and when. Following this step, a project manager is appointed and he calls upon various departments of the organization for the necessary specialized personnel. Most of these individuals are under his jurisdiction for the duration of the project, others merely lend a hand from time to time and remain in their respective departments. Additionally, the project manager has authority and responsibility for procuring materials, awarding sub-contracts, deciding procedures, establishing standards of performance and other activities necessary to carry out the project. Typically he is accountable

34

Figure 2
THE MATRIX ORGANIZATION
(Large engineering company—12 projects)

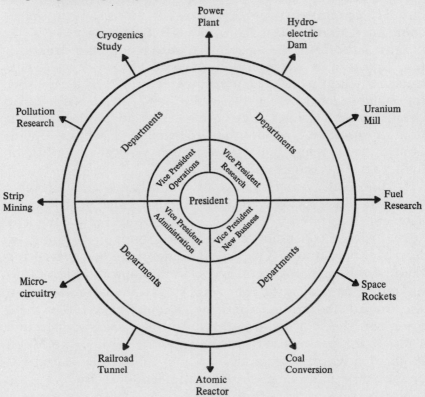

for quality, performance within the time schedule and profitability. At the termination of the project, employees temporarily assigned to him are returned to their respective departments.

Project teams can be utilized by an orthodox functional organization; matrix management is a continuing type of organization because of expectations that unique projects or research assignments will be repeated.

Successful use of the project team method, whether it is part of a traditional functional organization or is regular practice in a matrix organization, involves certain principles:

1. The objective must be specific and understood thoroughly by all members of the project.

2. The team members, combined, must provide all the knowledge and skill necessary to achieve the objective. They must be allowed to give their opinions, must cooperate with other members of the team yet be willing to subordinate their opinions to the judgment of the leader or to the achievement of the common goal. Sometimes a given member, because of wide knowledge or experience, becomes the actual leader of a project even though there is a nominal leader present.

3. Planning must be in great detail, and control devices set up. As the project unfolds, members should be kept informed through some system of feedback.

Frequently the project manager is more coordinator than director. Nevertheless, he must resolve conflicts or assert his authority if the program falls behind schedule. He must maintain a good relationship with heads of departments from which the members of this team have been drawn, and at the same time keep them from giving gratuitous instructions to his team members, which may conflict with his approach. At the close of the project he will be judged by what he *accomplished,* not by how well he planned, organized, coordinated, directed, or controlled, important as these elements are.

The project method of accomplishing given aims, and the matrix type of organization, accord with many of the findings of the behavioral sciences as to involvement and consultative relationships.

The executive council

Large companies are evolving a different kind of organization. These companies have discovered that the standard line and staff structure proves unwieldly, is too slow to react, and typically is unwilling to take the initiative. It sometimes promotes empire building which results in confusion or conflict. Moreover the burden of heading up a large company is often too great for any one man. Some companies try to resolve this by dividing top responsibility between the president and the chairman of the board, which is a move in the direction of the executive council. Figure 3 shows an executive council interposed between the normal functional departments and

36

Figure 3
THE EXECUTIVE COUNCIL

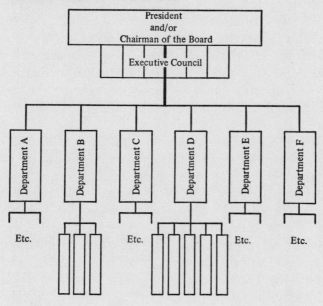

the president. Department heads consult with, but do not report to members of the council. This chart shows a council consisting of eight vice presidents, but some councils include the president and chairman of the board as well.

The council considers the problems and interrelationships among *all* functions of the business, although its members may be specialists in the various functions. Staff departments will report at various levels as in the normal functional chart. If the *staff* departments are corporate-wide in scope, they may report to the appropriate member of the advisory council, and not to a line manager. For example, an audit staff may report to the vice president of finance who is a member of the council. If the scope of the staff is confined to a function or sub-function, it may report to the appropriate line executive.

The advisory council will prepare long range plans, including the capital budget, for approval or revision by the corporate board of directors. However the preparation of the annual operating budget will begin at low levels with participation by supervisors or group leaders. Budgets will be integrated to successively higher levels. The advisory council will exercise strong control through budgets, through regular reports, and through charts. Each member of the advisory council has company-wide responsibility in his particular specialization. Thus, a vice president of research, and member of the council, could investigate research in any place in the organization and anyone engaged in research throughout the company is free to consult with him.

The large Du Pont Company has an executive council at the top. There is an executive committee of the board of directors that consists of six senior vice presidents, the president, and the Chairman of the Board, who also serves as chairman of the council. All are members of the board of directors; they are in effect a daily working board. The company believes that this approach strengthens group decision-making through objectivity and the utilization of varied viewpoints from individuals with varied knowledge and skills. Since those chosen for membership on the committee are at least ten years away from retirement at 65, there is a continuity of top-level administration. By relieving some of the burden on the chief executive, the executive committee encourages the resolution of problems at their own level or preferably at lower levels. In essence Du Pont's is the executive council type of organization at the top.

Small committees can be used at almost any organization level. They should however be utilized only when their joint effort can bring about a better result than the single manager could have done. A standing committee should understand clearly its scope, and the limitations to its authority. Its chairman should be selected for his ability to conduct meetings and prevent them from becoming perfunctory. An ad hoc committee will normally have a narrower objective and fewer meetings; it should be dissolved when either the objective has been accomplished or has been given up.

The grapevine

Sociologists—and wise managers, too—recognize the existence of a nebulous informal organization within a sizable formal organization. Its members have little status, its communication channels may be unusual, but it exercises considerable power over its members, for it may set the standards of conduct for the group.

In the summer between high school and college I worked as a runner for a bank. My job was to take envelopes around to various banks and get a receipt for them. In my youthful vigor I covered a lot of territory. However, about the third day an older employee took me aside and said with baleful emphasis, "We've all been watching you, and you are setting a bad example. From now on you are to cover no more than seven runs in a day. If you do more than seven, we're going to make it very unpleasant for you. Do you understand?" I understood!

The informal organization does not necessarily work against the interests of the formal organization. Some wise managers spot the leaders of the informal organization and use them for communication or ask their advice before undertaking change.

The ferment of change

In a dynamic organization, a great deal of reorganization takes place. Some of it results from quits, discharges, deaths, and transfers. Growth, innovation of products or methods, new ownership, or new top management usually cause a reshuffling of the organization. Sweeping reorganizations are likely to occur when there has been a prolonged period of falling sales or profits.

Too many organizational changes are designed merely to patch up some weakness that has appeared. Rather few have resulted from a comprehensive management audit designed to inventory the strong and weak points of an organization, ultimately transmuted into a long range plan of reorganization. If such an audit is intended to result in a reorganization program, virtually all key people who will be affected should be involved in the original fact gathering and in the development of the program itself. This approach takes more time than if the audit is done quietly by an outside consultant but involvement by the participants will usually ease the pangs of change and result in greater acceptance.

A company is a living entity and not a static fixture. Any company whose organization chart has not changed for a period of years is probably living in the past and not geared to the future. Properly planned change can prove self-renewing.

The right organization structure depends to a considerable extent on the nature of the problems to be solved as well as on the capabilities of the personnel available. The various types of organization structure can be placed on a continuum from highly centralized, functional (pyramidal) forms through executive councils to decentralized divisionals, to matrix types to projects and to production teams (discussed in a later chapter).

The pyramidal form of organization is generally found in mass production. Job shops require team effort. Process manufacturing, as in an oil refinery, requires a more formalized type of team effort. One-time unique projects usually will fare well in a matrix form of organization. Other factors that influence an organization structure are kind of ownership, size, rate of growth, attitudes of top executives, social pressures, political environments, and technological change.

In the current period of rapid change there is and will continue to be, need for knowledgeable specialists in organization theory in universities, government, and business.

Tomorrow's actions—NOW

Adapt your organizational structure primarily to the company's problems, but modified by the personal traits of top executives.

List the "growing pains" you have observed in your organization and note what should be done about them.

Press for further delegation at all levels—including your own.

If your company decentralized further, sketch the most likely organization chart. What top policies and practices would have to be changed?

Compare the formal organization chart of your company against actual reporting relationships (or their absence).

In your company, name the principal employees who exercise power in the "informal organization."

Quietly list key people of all levels able to handle higher responsibilities, showing age and other qualifications.

List three examples of needless "red tape" in your company.

Identify possible future situations where ad hoc task forces might perform better than the existing organization.

If you are part of a huge corporation, consider how an "executive council" could function.

Describe the present "management system"—the interrelationships among capital, plant, equipment, groups, leadership, delegation, and information flow. If starting afresh, how would you change any of them?

part two

*People will still be the most
important factor*

4

The new breed
Change is in the air

A few years ago, while traveling in England, I encountered a striking example of management's failure to understand worker psychology. As a service to employees, the manager of a company had contracted with a food supplier to send carts with food, sweets, tea, and coffee through the plant. Heretofore, employees had taken their tea break by going outside the plant. They refused to accept the new way, saying it was an invasion of their rights, and threatened to strike.

MANAGEMENT tomorrow must show greater understanding of a changed, and changing, work force. In this chapter we shall explore some of the factors that are bringing about the new conditions:

1. Age is one important factor. Fifty percent of the U.S. population is under 28 years of age. In the work force the figure is probably 30 to 35 percent. This ebullient generation has grown up under the influence of affluence, has had no ego-shaking contact with a severe business depression, despite a few short "recessions."

At the other end of the age spectrum are men and women who are living out already defeated lives—workers overwhelmed by life's pressures, who plod along toil-beaten paths to obscurity, are dismayed by the swirl of change that surrounds them.

Between these two age extremes lies a largely conservative group, acceptant of life, and puzzled by (and even somewhat envious of) the libertarianism and antics of younger workers.

2. The family is no longer a closely-knit group. Each member pursues his or her own interests, many of these outside the home. The father is no longer an authoritarian figure. Discipline of children is lax, or absent.

3. People of all ages and religious upbringing tend to be skeptical of organized religion and its conflicting tenets. The church building is no longer a social center. The young, particularly, are turned off by obvious hypocrisy of their elders and by political corruption.

4. More people are getting more education, even among minority groups. Many employees are better educated than their bosses; this situation undoubtedly lessens respect for constituted authority.

5. Affluence satisfies most of the basic wants—food, clothing, shelter. Union demands for higher pay, combined with shortages of employable labor, have increased both earnings and economic security. Inflation, too! Pressure groups and unions attract civil service employees, school teachers, nurses, technicians and semi-professionals.

6. Legislation, also, adds to earnings, security, and health. Witness minium wage and hour laws, equal employment opportunity, OSHA and similar enactments.

7. Federal, state and local welfarism of various kinds may make it almost as lucrative not to work as to work, so shifting the production burden to those who continue in their jobs.

8. Nationwide communication reduces the insularity of workers—radio, television, newspapers, magazines. Wage rates and fringe benefits become common knowledge. Left-leaning writers, teachers, and broadcasters sometimes weep crocodile tears for the "poor, downtrodden worker," who enjoys the highest standard of living in the entire world.

9. The automobile has contributed, by providing employees greater mobility in job-hopping and in use of free time. Gasoline shortages, however, are providing limitations.

As a consequence of these and other influences the so-called work ethic plays a less important part in the lives of most employees. The only time some of them work like a horse is when the boss is riding them! More leisure is the "in thing."

Part of the demand for leisure is illustrated by the "coffee break," a world-wide phenomenon. One Australian employer posted this notice:

> "Starting January 1, a new policy known as the work break will be inaugurated. It is hoped that employees will try to fit this into their already busy schedule of coffee breaks, rest periods, vacations, and days off."

A Gallup poll revealed that, overall, 19 percent of American workers are unhappy in their jobs—but 33 percent of those 18 to 29 years old consider their jobs unsatisfactory. Asked whether they could produce more, 52 percent of all workers answered yes, but 70 percent of young workers gave this same answer.

Other nations are experiencing much the same condition as we. British life has become one of the most permissive —and chaotic—in the entire world. Even in communist Russia, the winds of change are straining at the guyropes of Leninist oligarchy. Author Vance Packard believes that a breakdown in community living augmented by greater mobility, is largely responsible for attitudes of the "now generation." A French writer, Jean Francois Revel, says that America is in the vanguard of the second world revolution, characterized by freedom of dissent and wide access to great stores of information. If these observers prove right, great opportunities for a new leadership lie ahead.

New employee attitudes

Sen. Charles H. Percy (R–Ill.) speaking before the National Conference on the Changing Work Ethic said,

> Outside the plant gate or office door is the new American: a future-oriented, demanding, expectant, educated, freedom-loving individual. Inside that gate or door this interesting, creative, inventive American is required to conform to a past-

oriented, authoritarian, hierarchical, class-based, freedom-fearing social system. Thus, in spite of more pay and benefits than ever before, all kinds of working men and women, "blue collar" and "white collar," are unhappy in their work—unhappy and unfulfilled in a large and important part of their lives. The costs to our society of increasing worker frustration are only beginning to be studied, but there is some evidence that profound dissatisfaction with work has a kind of polluting effect on the larger society.

"Blue-collar blues" is the catch-phrase used by writers to describe the new attitudes of many workers. It implies dissatisfaction of employees with their jobs, and such dissatisfaction affects white collar and managerial employees as well, yielding "white collar willies."

Since only about 2 percent of people at work are on production assembly lines, we must look beyond such lines for causes of discontent. It is also true that more than 50% of workers are engaged in non-manufacturing activities.

Some researchers assert that employees are no more alienated from their jobs than their fathers were before them.

A.A. Imberman, a management consultant, surveyed 3,800 factory employees in five states; all were assembly workers. He found that 80 percent had no complaint about repetitive operations on the assembly line. Things which worried them were, principally, bad supervision; poor scheduling; working conditions—machines, tools, lighting, ventilation, crowded floors; management policies; and lack of involvement in job related problems.

Since I have conducted several hundred employee attitude surveys over two decades, I give the following considered opinions on this controversial subject:

1. Employees *are* less interested in work, quality, regular attendance, and company success.

2. They crave more feeling of worthwhileness, express their job (and outside) frustrations in demands for more money.

3. They respond well to less bossism, more freedom of action in their jobs, and to greater challenge.

Although employees express their discontent in terms of

money, earnings can scarcely be blamed. A General Motors employee, for example, averages well over $5.00 per hour and receives fringe benefits equivalent to an additional 25 percent. His job may be to install a time-studied number of right front wheels every hour, 40 hours per week. Despite pay and benefits, GM employees manifest their unhappiness in strikes, absenteeism, turnover, indifference, and sabotage. Management denies that employees suffer from "blue-collar blues," labeling the term a press fiction. As though to belie its own words, the company promotes a movie that attempts to show that workers aren't bored!

Strikes typically yield higher pay for organized workers and add to inflation, but fail to improve job satisfactions. Frequently wages lost during a strike are not recovered by an increase won; union members are beginning to get this message. Likewise, society in general is becoming fed up with the power of organized groups to paralyze large communities to serve their own ends.

Newsweek Feature Service quoted Arnold Gridson, a behavior specialist, as follows:

> There's no question about it. There is a major transformation under way in worker attitudes toward the whole concept of work. And it's by no means limited to blue-collar workers. . . . It's wrong to say workers are slothful and indifferent today. It's just the opposite. They want to do satisfying work.

Data reveal lowered morale

Loss of worker enthusiasm is showing up in production figures; some managers feel that employees stop looking for work when they find a good job.

To study the problem, the American Management Association organized a meeting on "Productivity Improvement—a Top Challenge to Human Resources Development." Some highlights:

1. Between 1965 and 1970, U.S. industrial productivity increased only 10 percent, compared with 40 to 90 percent in other advanced countries.

2. One manufacturer reported that, over a four-year

period, his labor turnover had increased 70 percent and absenteeism 50 percent.

3. The Gallup poll, previously cited, reported that 54 percent of blue-collar workers (as distinct from all employees) admitted that they could accomplish more if they tried—more than half of them said by 20 percent.

4. Job enrichment and consultative relationships do not eliminate the need for output goals or production standards.

Above I have mentioned the attitude surveys our consulting organization has conducted over several decades. Throughout this period we have noted a steady deterioration in percentages of favorable responses. Some companies have had us do repeat surveys every four years. Despite the fact that these are well managed concerns, the same deterioration has appeared. We have had to conclude that the worsening morale results both from forces beyond the control of management, as well as from management's failure to understand the true nature of the problem. Moreover, there is often a wide gap between the splendor of a company personnel policy and its sullied application at the employee level.

Our surveys reveal that the loss of morale is not confined to blue-collar workers. We find it in clerical employees, technical employees and supervisors. Its principal manifestations are labor turnover, absenteeism, loafing, prolonged coffee breaks, grievances, indifference to quality, insubordination, and even sabotage. In later chapters we shall consider some things managers can do to lessen the impact of these negative employee reactions.

We should here note that:

1. No undeniable statistical proof exists that a satisfied employee is a higher producer than one who manifests continuing discontent. The latter does, however, contribute to absenteeism, labor turnover, conflict, and strikes.

2. Those who believe that present-day workers are no more alienated from jobs than was true years ago assert that the very same things are bothering workers: accident hazards, faulty equipment, poor ventilation, abusive foremen and, above all, lack of opportunity to get ahead.

The plight of many hourly workers is epitomized in the statements made to me by an intelligent machinist: "When I graduated from high school, I entered a four year apprentice program, and later completed a correspondence course in tool-making. Now I'm the highest paid mechanic in our shop, but I'll never go any higher here. Company policy is to hire college trained engineers as foremen and move them up. If I can get financial backing, I'm going to start my own job shop."

On-the-job frustration

Much labor turnover, particularly in lower level jobs, results from disappointment. Perhaps the employment interviewer or the foreman has painted a rosy picture of the task or of its opportunities. Once on the job, the employee finds some black smudges in the picture. Fellow employees prove diffident or antagonistic. The previously friendly foreman-interviewer develops a seamy side. The work is harder than stated, or just plain boring. Promotions or pay increases fail to materialize, as expected. The employee who started the new job with high hopes gradually suffers disillusionment. If he can get a job somewhere else he takes it, chasing a will-o'-the-wisp job happiness. If he can't or won't change jobs, he may resign himself to fate, bearing the frustrations in exchange for the pay envelope.

> Our attitude surveys reveal a U-shaped morale curve: high during the first year of employment; falling for the next four years; slowly rising after the fifth year. Those who couldn't adjust to their jobs and company have long since quit or been fired. In most companies, it takes ten years for the curve to again reach the first year level.

Psychologists have frequently pointed out that a job frustrating to one employee is satisfying to another.

> Some years ago I was in the plant of a cosmetics company, standing beside a slow-moving conveyor line where six girls filled, packed and labeled ladies' compacts. One of the six girls was leaving that day because she "couldn't stand the monotony of the job." That same day the foreman interviewed a former employee who had left to be married. She wanted her

old job back because she "couldn't stand the monotony of housework."

Certain attributes of jobs and their encumbents normally contribute to boredom. Figure 4, Rating of Job Attributes, can help you as a manager determine which jobs under your supervision are most likely to be frustrating to the average worker. This determination may help you understand job dissatisfaction among some of your subordinates.

Other interesting findings from our employee attitude surveys are that small companies generally enjoy higher morale than large companies; apparently employees feel lost in giant organizations. Graveyard (night) shifts usually have better morale than day shifts; night shifts are typically small groups, with considerable inter-dependence among their members.

These proven findings lend support to the idea of small teams in production instead of highly specialized solo tasks on a continuous assembly line.

In addition to the above rating of job attributes, it may be an interesting exercise to rate your company on some of its personnel practices. Figure 5, "Rating of Company on Personnel Practices," permits you to rate your department, plant or company on ten significant factors. This form has never been standardized; it is offered as an analytic way of evaluating various personnel policies and practices. However, the author has used this form in enough situations to believe that the standards shown at the bottom of the rating form are reasonable. The words "satisfier" and "dissatisfier" will be made clear to you in Chapter 6.

Drugs and alcoholism

A survey of 128 companies revealed that alcoholism and drug usage among industrial employees were increasing at an alarming rate.[1] This study suggested that almost 50 percent

---

[1] Reported in a study, *Drug Abuse and Your Company*, by Susan Halpern, American Management Association, 135 W. 50 St., N.Y., N.Y. 10020. The cost is $11.50.

Figure 4
RATING OF JOB ATTRIBUTES

Job _____ Date _____
Employee _____ Rater_____

Below are ten attributes. Five are characteristics of the work itself, five pertain to the employee on the job (or to a typical employee).

Each attribute has five possible gradations. Check the one that is most closely applicable to this job.

1. Repetitiveness
   a. One simple repetitive operation
   b. Series of operations repeated sequentially
   c. Several different operations, repeated
   d. Variety of operations, some repeated
   e. Each task different
2. Time from beginning to end of operation
   a. 5 seconds or less
   b. 6 to 59 seconds
   c. 1 to 5 minutes
   d. 6 to 60 minutes
   e. More than one hour
3. Machine operations
   a. Operates one or more automatic machines
   b. Feeds one machine manually
   c. Sets up, then feeds one or more machines manually
   d. Varied machines used as needed.
   e. Does not operate any machine
4. Worker is supplied with work:
   a. Every 5 seconds or less
   b. 6 to 59 seconds
   c. 1 to 5 minutes
   d. 6 to 60 minutes
   e. No set time for task completion
5. Learning time for proficiency
   a. One day or less
   b. 2 to 5 days
   c. 6 to 21 days (*i.e.*, one month)
   d. 2 to 6 months
   e. More than 6 months
6. Typical or actual age of worker
   a. Under 20
   b. 20 to 24
   c. 25 to 29
   d. 30 to 39
   e. 40 and over
7. Typical or actual length of service
   a. Under 1 week
   b. 1 to 4 weeks
   c. 1 to 5 months
   d. 6 to 23 months
   e. 2 years or more
8. Typical or actual earnings
   a. Minimum hourly wage
   b. Low, below average
   c. Average of shop or plant
   d. High, above average
   e. Among three highest
9. Immediate boss's attitude is
   a. Harsh or critical
   b. Stern
   c. Impersonal but fair
   d. Friendly
   e. Like a team coach
10. Fellow workers are
    a. Full of dissension
    b. Sullen
    c. Indifferent
    d. Mostly cooperative
    e. Friendly and helpful

To summarize, allow 1 point for all "a" checks, 2 for "b," 3 for "c," 4 for "d," and 5 for "e." Total and refer to the following table:

Total points	Significance
10 to 19	Probably a frustrating job
20 to 27	Monotonous or boring
28 to 32	Just a job for the money
33 to 40	Some interesting aspects
41 to 50	Should be satisfying

Figure 5
RATING OF COMPANY ON PERSONNEL PRACTICES

Rate the usual conditions in your plant or company as to the following ten factors by placing a check mark in the block that comes closest to your opinion. If you can't decide between two blocks, check the narrow space between them. Only *one* check in each line!

Motivator (satisfier) factors — *Points*

Factor									
1—Making work interesting	No organized company effort **B4**	**C6**	Some departmental effort **U8**	**X10**	Flexible hours for some jobs **C12**	**X14**	Use of tests and career counseling **F16**	**H18**	Strong program of job enrichment **D20**
2—Employee involvement	Strict, impersonal supervision **E4**	**Q6**	Mostly weak supervision **A8**	**V10**	Good personal supervision **D12**	**Y14**	Consultative relationships on goals and methods **G18**	**J16**	Production teams with considerable autonomy **A20**
3—Employee development	No management concern with this problem **O2**	**T3**	Hit-or-miss development on the job **F4**	**R5**	Occasional stab at organized training **B6**	**Z7**	Well organized, continuing program **N8**	**P9**	Development program pushed by top management **H10**
4—Giving recognitions	Criticism only **S3**	**A5**	Penalty system for errors **P6**	**U8**	Neutral—neither penalties nor rewards **G9**	**S11**	Titles and other status symbols **D12**	**K14**	Repeated public recognition for achievements **C15**
5—Delegation	Autocratic management **A2**	**R3**	Responsibility without authority delegated **T4**	**B5**	Some minor authority is delegated **Q6**	**V7**	In some departments, delegation done properly **H8**	**L9**	Enforced systematic program of delegation **D10**

Hygiene (dissatisfier) factors

Factor									
6—Relationships	Employees hostile to supervisors **J1**	**E2**	Unfriendliness among employees **B2**	**A3**	Indifference throughout the organization **U3**	**C4**	Attitude of friendliness prevails **R4**	**O5**	Supervisors provide good leadership **C5**
7—Salary and fringe benefits	Many earnings inequities **E1**	**J2**	Meagre fringe benefits **K2**	**F3**	Average earnings and benefits **C3**	**E4**	Earnings well above average of community **V4**	**D5**	Excellent wage and salary administration **L5**
8—Company personnel policies	No established policies **J1**	**O2**	Policies are long since out of date **F2**	**K3**	Management allows too many exceptions **L3**	**G4**	Good policies consistently observed **D4**	**R5**	Written policies upheld; revised as indicated **A5**
9—Security	Frequent erratic layoffs **N1**	**S2**	Seasonal layoffs **K2**	**P3**	"Even the bums don't get fired" **G3**	**L4**	Year-around stable employment **N4**	**H5**	Profitable growth company needs more employees **G5**
10—Working conditions	Many unprotected hazards **P1**	**T2**	Unpleasant surroundings **O2**	**B3**	Acceptable working conditions **L3**	**Q4**	Mostly above average **H4**	**N5**	Excellent lighting, atmosphere and safety **R5**

To score your ratings, credit the points shown in each block or space; ignore the letters. Refer total points to the following table:

Total points	Significance
90 to 100	Outstanding showing
76 to 89	Alert to change
52 to 75	Usual; traditional
34 to 51	Needs new thinking
20 to 33	Very low standing

Total points _____

of industrial employees are victims of alcohol or drugs. Sociologists believe that much of this condition is attributable to work frustration. Some wag has suggested that overindulgence in alcohol can give you a red nose, a white liver, a yellow streak, a dark brown breath, and a blue outlook.

New study

The Department of Health, Education and Welfare has produced a controversial report on the causes of, and remedies for, employee apathy and frustration. It holds that industrial management is partially responsible for various manifestations of employee dissatisfaction: alcoholism, drug abuse, illness, depression, aggression, sabotage, absenteeism, turnover, and poor quality of work. It contends that today's better educated, young employees, will not tolerate routinized jobs they consider degrading and unchallenging, despite high pay and good working conditions. The assembly line gets much of the criticism.

The authors of the report accept the recommendations of a number of sociologists. These recommendations include:

1. Worker participation in decisions affecting their jobs— time standards, working methods, tools, new machines, etc.;
2. Greater responsibility on employees for production and quality; less supervision;
3. Profit sharing;
4. Job enrichment;
5. Group production;
6. Project teams;
7. Job rotation;
8. Vested pension rights; and
9. Job retraining.

These proposed solutions will be considered in later chapters.

Unemployment figures

Study of unemployment data since 1900 shows the following approximate figures:

Decade	Av. %	High %	Low %
1900–1909	5	7	2
1910–1919	5	9	2
1920–1929	4	11	2
1930–1939	13	25	3
1940–1949	5	17	1
1950–1959	5	6	3
1960–1969	5	6	5
1970–1979	5 (est.)	—	—

Note that in recent decades, the figures have been fairly stable.

Unemployment currently hovers around 5 to 6 percent of the work force, even as industry decries labor shortages. This seeming anomaly is readily explained by an analysis of the situation. In many communities the unemployed are largely unskilled youths, minority workers or women with no skills in great demand. Some persons are unemployable because of age or physical condition. Skilled workers, unemployed, are scarce, or may live in a locality where their particular skills are not in demand.

In recent years, more than 25 percent of the unemployed have been under the age of 20. Industry or society, or both, face a large vocational training problem, especially for minority members.

Actually the 5 to 6 percent unemployment figure means little. The age, sex, skill, and color mix at any given time is as significant as the overall figure. In many communities, the scarcity of skilled and semi-skilled workers undoubtedly aggravates absenteeism, labor turnover and indifference to quality. Harried managers try to convince employees that these practices are killing the goose that lays the golden eggs, so far with indifferent results. Apparently, other motivations are needed.

Economic recessions cause employees to stick closer to their jobs, but this cure is harsh. Labor shortages may be eased in the decade ahead by a large bulge in available workers in the 25 to 34 age group.

What the crystal ball shows

This book makes no claim to oracular divination. But, in the opinion of the author, until or unless some of the ideas brought out in this book are put into new and better practices, American industry can expect only worsening of existing trends; people at work, different from prior generations, will increasingly be a management headache. Man has been wasteful of many resources—including human resources.

Labor shortages will likely remain, leading to more capital expenditures for more automated equipment. The operation of such equipment may, in turn, lead to more employee frustration.

Supervisors at all levels will adopt different tactics in handling subordinates. The boss will wrap a cloak of tact around naked criticism, will coach rather than demand, consult rather than command.

Training of young minority workers should greatly accelerate. This training will take advantage of programmed instruction and computer-controlled instruction.

Since the likelihood of stopping inflation seems remote, the wage demands of workers may well accelerate, and the result will be more inflation. Conceivably we could price ourselves out of international competition, despite the fact that most industrialized nations reveal greater inflation than ours.

A growing number of working wives are "bringing home the bacon." The Census Bureau reported that in 1970, there were 44 million husband-wife families; by now the figure is greater. In three million of the 1970 families, the wives earned more than the husbands. Of all working wives, 22 percent were in clerical occupations and 21 percent in professional or technical fields. The female percentage of the total working force in 1973 was approximately 38 percent, and rising each year. The reasons they give for working are income and "to get out of the house," rather than job challenge or career fulfillment.

Employers will be more concerned about skill, experience, intelligence, interests, and attitudes of employees than about their years of formal education. Talent inventories will be maintained.

Individual incentive pay plans will gradually give way to group bonuses, profit sharing, and plant wide plans—rewards for measurable *results*. Employee ownership of company stock will increase.

Many conveyor and assembly line jobs will be regrouped into logical production centers, operated by teams. Team members will perform a variety of operations, in some cases rotating jobs to relieve monotony and to add to employee versatility and for job enrichment. Repetitive, non-assembly line jobs will likewise benefit from job enrichment.

Employees will seek, and get, greater participation in matters that affect them or their jobs.

Managers will reluctantly accept findings of social scientists.

Under legislative suasion, employers will provide more health care and other fringe benefits to employees.

Union leaders will suffer more disaffection of members; will become more socially responsible; will cooperate more with management.

Flexible working hours will come into greater use, as will the four day workweek.

Unemployment will not change materially, will continue to vary inversely with the business cycle.

Not all these changes will occur at the same time; some may never come about; some will be altered by political or economic events as yet not visioned. What is important to realize is that since workers have changed, work must change. In succeeding chapters we shall examine our predictions in some detail.

Tomorrow's actions—NOW

Take numerous constructive actions to develop your employees of all levels.

Base actions on the realization that young workers, fresh from high school or college, resist management regimentation, seek more freedom of decision and action.

Analyze statistics of your workforce—by sex, age, length of

service, education, jobs, turnovers, etc. Compare data against the status five or ten years ago to note changes.

Inventory the abilities of female and minority employees.

Provide promotion opportunities to competent women and minority workers.

Place greater stress on job training at the lower levels.

Determine what different approaches you need to manage your "knowledge workers."

Identify different employee attitudes and actions over those that existed 10 or 20 years ago.

Periodically, get an employee attitude survey to note changes and trends in departments, age groups, sex, etc.

5

People problems are here to stay

We shall here consider the following problems: labor shortages, labor turnover, absenteeism, and compensation and fringe benefits.

Overcoming labor shortages

In most industrial communities there is an acute shortage of semi-skilled and skilled labor. At the same time many of these areas have an unemployment rate well above the national average. Although the basic problem revolves around the word "skilled," there are other contributing factors, such as employer reluctance to train the unskilled, reliance on futile pirating of employees from other employers, higher technical requirements for operators of automated equipment, union limitations on apprenticeship, union jurisdictional disputes, generous unemployment and welfare benefits, bungling governmental bureaucracy, inadequacies of educational facilities, absenteeism, and increasing worker indifference. Available evidence suggests that the labor shortage problem will become more acute in the decade ahead.

In the hope of achieving a higher economic level, many communities are aggressively seeking new plants. Yet it must be obvious that the availability of labor and particularly of skilled labor, is one of the first considerations of a company contemplating a new plant location. Since most states face this same dilemma, the problem assumes national dimensions.

The usual reaction of an employer who loses a skilled worker is that he must get a replacement at all costs. So he lures away such a worker from a nearby company by offering a substantial wage increase. In retaliation the other company may return the compliment. All the while both employers are complaining that "We're the training ground for other companies," or "We had to steal that worker or shut down the production line," or "If that's the game they want to play, we can play it too."

Playing "musical chairs" with skilled workers merely increases labor costs, doesn't increase total production a bit, makes a lot of loyal employees unhappy, and induces absenteeism and labor turnover.

This situation has become so acute that some *communities* are raiding other communities to lure skilled labor away. This practice leads to a dog-eat-dog existence, which in the long run fosters inflation and benefits neither the pirating employers nor their respective communities.

In the previous chapter we talked about changing attitudes toward work, particularly toward manual work. This situation is clearly illustrated in the scarcity of short-order cooks, housemaids and gardeners—occupations that could be recruited from many unemployed workers who will seek unemployment benefits rather than endure the social stigma of being a "menial."

Each company should analyze its shortage problem. Is it in the laboring group, the semi-skilled or the skilled? What specific jobs are causing the trouble? This analysis enables a company to attack its specific problems rather than the situation in general.

The next step is to analyze in writing the requirements of each job in which shortages are occurring. Such an analysis should indicate the duties as well as the mental, skill, and physical requirements, the working conditions, the specific responsibilities and the kind of supervision provided. This information leads to:

1. Possible "deskilling" some jobs so that they require less experience from new employees; more difficult duties are turned over to present experienced employees.

2. Preparation of hiring specifications to guide the employment interviewer or outside employment agency.

3. Specific job training, possibly of minority applicants.

Increased automation of many manufacturing processes has resulted in two contrary trends:

1. Some jobs are much easier to operate. For example, the operator in a bakery who merely watches a few dials does not need the skill of an oldtime baker.

2. Some jobs are more difficult and hence require more training. The programmer for an electronic computer provides an obvious example.

As skill is transferred from workers to machines, the training period for machine operators is shortened, and that for technicians is lengthened. In essence this means that the training of ideas is becoming more important than that of senses and muscles. As technology advances, our greatest labor shortages will be in jobs which require technically *informed* workers. At the moment however, companies are faced with a shortage of workers trained in the manipulative skills needed for performance of certain manual or machine-paced specialized tasks.

Alert employers will look ahead to the implications of technology in their respective industries and institute steps to insure that a sufficient supply of *well informed* workers will be available. The problem goes deeper than appears on the surface. It is a nationwide socio-psycho-economic situation that will not be solved by practice training alone, although in-plant training can alleviate the problem for most employers. Beyond the actions of an individual employer lie joint employer actions in given communities, with education and government sharing responsibility. The shortage of knowledgeable technologists is national, not local.

There are four principal avenues through which management can undertake to overcome its skilled worker shortages.

Briefly these avenues are selection, training, motivation, and supervision.

The analyses of jobs, mentioned above, can be of value in all four of these approaches, especially in selection and training. In this chapter we shall consider these two only.

Selection

The improvement of selection begins with the sources of labor supply. Here are some typical sources: applicants to the employment department; friends of present employees; newspaper ads; employment agencies; schools, churches, and social agencies; societies and associations; unions; minority groups; retirees in good health; handicapped persons; and last but not least, present employees.

Many progressive employers are using tests in selection. Any company that fails to do so runs the risk that it will get applicants who have been rejected by other employers or it will fail to pick up an occasional diamond-in-the-rough who may not handle himself well in an interview but who nevertheless has considerable capacity.

Legislation, administrative interpretations, and a Supreme Court decision have put a premium upon employers to validate their tests. In essence the word validation means to prove that a test measures abilities that are required for job performance. There are various degrees of sophistication in validating tests. One of the simplest is to compare test scores of those who make out well on a given job against those who do poorly or who fail. If the averages of the two groups are vastly different you have an indication that the test is valid. Another method is job sampling. Perhaps the task is to gauge metal parts with a "go no-go" guage. Applicants are shown how to use the gauge and are given a number of metal parts to gauge against a certain time limit. If you have previously determined that your competent employees gauge more in a given period of time than the incompetent, you have an indication of validation. Many personnel managers have been trained in a more sophisticated statistical method of test validation known as correlation.

Employment tests can be classified into two general types: tests of capacity to learn a job and tests of acquired proficiency in a given occupation.

The principal kinds of employment tests are as follows:

1. General intelligence. It will screen out applicants with low capacity to absorb idea training. However it is likely to discriminate against minority applicants who in their early years have been "culturally deprived."

2. Dexterity tests will screen out those who are poorly coordinated in muscular movements or who have a slow reaction time. There are numerous tests available for manual dexterity.

3. Information, performance, and picture tests are useful for applicants who claim ability in a given field. Stenographic and accounting tests would be examples, as would tests of technical information in scores of specialized fields.

4. Clerical tests will guage speed and accuracy in typical clerical activities such as filing, classifying, mathematics, or visual comparisons.

5. Interest tests can gauge whether an applicant likes to work with people, mathematics, ideas, or physical objects. Or they may show predilection for certain fields such as mechanics, persuasion, or clerical.

Eye testing equipment will detect astigmatism, vertical or lateral imbalance, poor depth perception, color blindness, nearsightedness, or farsightedness. An audiometer will detect loss of ability to hear sounds of certain frequencies. The Occupational Safety and Health Act (OSHA) contains penalties for employers who violate its noise standards. Tests are available that register the strength of hand grip, of leg muscles, of back muscles, and of lung capacity. These are all physiological tests which should not require validation.

Employment tests do better in rejecting applicants than in selecting them. If an applicant flunks a test that has been proven to correlate with job success (*i.e.*, validated), his chances of succeeding, if employed, will be low. However the fact that he passes the test does not automatically guarantee that he will succeed; too many other factors not measured by the tests may cause his failure.

Tests should be used as a supplement to interviewing, not a substitute for it. A good interviewer will bring out educational, experiential, and social backgrounds of the applicant. He will try to determine the attitude of the applicant toward the employing company and particularly toward the kind of work the applicant would be required to do if employed. The work success of parents, brothers and sisters will be considered, as well as the applicant's economic and career objectives. These items become increasingly important with high level vacancies.

Former employers know more about your applicant than you can know with all your tests and interviews. Frequently they are reluctant to reduce such knowledge to writing, so if you really want to know how an applicant has performed in the past, go see his former bosses, or talk with them by telephone.

The physical examination by a doctor may prevent hiring an applicant with a deficiency that could interfere with job performance. However don't hesitate to hire handicapped persons where such interference does not exist—they will usually prove to be excellent employees.

Some companies have found that it pays to let an applicant watch the job before he accepts it, so he will understand the working conditions. Quite often this can be done at the time he is interviewed by the foreman or other prospective boss.

Scarcity of applicants should not deter you from being careful in selection. Carelessness will only cause you to fill the same jobs again and again.

We have found that an internal search for talent will usually reveal some present employees with talents or interests of use to a company. Under this plan, employees are invited to volunteer for aptitude testing. To avoid a suspicion of bias, each volunteer is assigned a number, which number is known only to him and to the personnel manager. Those who volunteer are given a test of general intelligence and two tests of vocational interests. The three tests are scored and those who do reasonably well are given further tests along lines of their revealed interests. After this they are interviewed at some length, taking into account education, experience and work history with the company. Typically a search for talent, properly publicized, will reveal about 5 percent of the working force with abilities and interests of greater value to the employer than in their present assignments. Sometimes it prevents the separation of an employee who is "a square peg in a round hole."

Since shortage of skilled labor appears to be a "problem with a future," far-seeing managers will utilize all analytic selection devices available.

Training

One value of training, particularly on-the-job training, is that it obviates the necessity for finding new employees. Job analyses and employment tests are excellent preliminary steps for on-the-job training, whether given by a skilled employee, by a special instructor or by a foreman.

Experience has shown that short periods of instruction with practice are better than prolonged training. Frequently neglected is the idea of imparting *meaning* to the trainee. Jobs have a reason for being; they fit into the scheme of things. Understanding the significance of a job adds motivation.

> During a war period, a colonel was put in charge of a plant that manufactured airplane engines. When the first engine that came off the line had been installed in an airplane, he had the plane flown off from the plant grounds. All employees were given an hour off to watch the demonstration and a great cheer arose when the plane was airborne. The colonel had added meaning to the manufacture of airplane engines.

Learning does not develop at a constant pace. The trainee spurts upward for a time, seems to be improving well; then he hits a "plateau" where he ceases to advance or even falls backward for a time. Apparently these plateaus are periods of absorption when what has been learned is being digested in preparation for a new spurt forward. Plateaus are more observable with idea training than with sensory or muscle training.

Much of what a novice has been told or shown is forgotten withing a short period after the telling or showing. To remedy this situation, a trainer should see that the novice learns through as many senses as possible and has an opportunity to repeat the knowledge or motion.

There are two guiding principles used in training work:

1. Proceed from the known to the unknown. Application of this principle requires that the trainer understands what the trainee does, and does not, know.

2. Proceed from the simple to the complex, to achieve some difficult skill or integrated body of knowledge.

Many companies have had considerable success with programmed instruction. The term refers to so-called "teaching machines" or to specially constructed books that:

1. Present fractions of the material to be learned, in ascending order of difficulty and in relationship one to another. These fractions may be information to be memorized, pictures to be comprehended, problems to be solved or tasks to be performed.

2. Give the trainee a way to respond, typically by checking one of a number of choices offered him by a multiple choice presentation, or by pressing certain response keys.

3. Give him immediate feedback as to the correctness of his response, so permitting him to go on to the next frame of a viewer, or to the next page, as a "reward."

4. Keep his attention concentrated on the material to be learned.

5. Permit him to progress at his own pace.

The success of this kind of instruction depends on the programming; *i.e.*, the prior analysis of what is to be learned so that it leads the trainee from the known to the unknown, and from the simple to the complex. Programmed instruction can be either individual or group. If it is the latter, sufficient machines or texts must be available for group members, even though each member may be learning at his own pace.

Another approach to solving the problem of labor shortage is to deskill higher level tasks, mentioned above. The experienced machine operator sets up work for inexperienced new employees; the engineer is given an estimating clerk; the chemist, a laboratory assistant; the salesman, a detailer; the foreman, a shop clerk. This device enables experienced people to function at a higher level than if they are required to spend time on lower level tasks.

Where a given job performs two distinctly different duties, it may be possible to assign one whole duty to another employee. Thus the tax work may be taken away from the office manager; market research from the sales manager; quality control from the foreman; the storeroom from the purchasing agent; new product research from the chief engineer, etc.

Both horizontal and vertical splitting of jobs, described above, assume that a sufficiently intelligent person is available to take on the duties and that adequate training will be given to him. In this approach, companies should consider their intelligent female employees, many of whom are quite capable of taking on higher level tasks.

In most communities there is an abundance of people with brainpower even though they may not yet be trained to take on some of the specialized technologies which are emerging. Likewise, a comprehensive search for talent in your company will usually discover such individuals in the ranks. If your company fails to employ young people of potential talent, it will ultimately suffer from a paucity of such persons. Incentives will not create talent; no amount of whipping will convert dray horses into race horses.

Reducing labor turnover

Many of the management actions listed above for attracting employees or otherwise solving labor shortages are applicable in reducing labor turnover. Turnover in many companies is larger than most managers believe or are willing to admit. Since much of it occurs in a few low level jobs, managers normally do not consider the problem critical, especially if new employees can be taught the simple duties within a few days. Hence the accent is on finding employees, rather than on reducing turnover.

A simple formula for calculating your monthly labor turnover percentage is as follows:

$$\text{Percentage of turnover} = \frac{\text{the number of separations}}{\text{the average number on the payroll}} \times 100$$

To convert this figure to an annual basis, multiply by 12.

Another useful figure is the calculation of labor *persistence*. What percentage of your employees have been with you more than a year? Five years? Ten years? What is the average length of service for all employees? Annual calculation of these figures can reveal whether you are going ahead or falling behind in labor stability. When labor turnover involves a considerable number of skilled and semi-skilled operators, you're not just heading for trouble—you already have it.

Most personnel managers divide their labor turnover into voluntary and involuntary categories and become concerned when the "quit rate" increases. This silent strike, as it has been termed, means that employees are escaping something in the company to which they could not adjust.

Typically, at time of leaving, employees tell the boss that they are "getting more money" elsewhere, but researchers have discovered that this glib statement frequently masks a number of prior unhappy experiences, which caused the employee to search for another job or to be receptive to another offer Personnel departments frequently interview employees who are about to quit, to prevent the separation or to find reasons for it. Sometimes valuable information can be gleaned from this practice. On the other hand many of the simplistic reasons for leaving given by employees at the time of departure are untrue, only partially true or rational coverups for the real reasons.

> The comptroller of a well known mid-western company kept making passes at his secretary, a beautiful girl who was engaged to be married. When she quit her well paying job, the exit interviewer wrote on her personnel card, "Left to be married." He never knew the real reason nor the fact that she and her fiance did not plan to get married for another year. Hers was a rational coverup for the real reason.

A few companies have sent out investigators to interview former employees, in a search for real reasons.

Our organization made one such study for a large oil company. In addition to getting closer to the real reasons, we learned that a night foreman in the shipping department was padding the payroll with a fictitious shipping clerk; that a service station manager had devised an ingenious method of cheating fuel oil customers. In both these instances employees had left because they were afraid of being involved should the crookedness come to light.

Sometimes employees quit or are fired because they fail to meet standards of productivity or quality. Such a condition may result from basic incapacity or from lack of training. If an employee has been put on a job which demands more intellectual grasp, better muscular coordination, or faster reaction time than he possesses, the fault is the employers; these capacities could have been measured in the employment office. When such conditions are uncovered, the employer must decide whether to deskill the task, train the worker, or remove him from the job. Unfortunately most foremen see the problem differently—they say, "Either he produces or I get rid of him." In time of labor shortage this arbitrary viewpoint only aggravates the problem.

Some employees leave because of lack of interest in the work to be done. Extreme disinterest can lead to emotional frustration. Work interest means that an employee derives a feeling of satisfaction from the task and/or the surrounding circumstances. Previously in this chapter we have mentioned tests that determine areas of strong interest. An employee who has a strongly developed interest in one kind of work but who is forced into another will emotionally fight his job and will try to escape from it.

An excellent example comes to mind. While we were working with a midwestern machine tool company, a union shop steward was causing management a lot of trouble. When we conducted a search for talent he was one of the volunteers, finally revealing both interest in and ability with mathematics. When he was transferred from a job as internal grinder to manufacturing cost accountant, his whole personality pattern changed for the better.

Employers in the future, understanding the discontent that comes from work that violates an employee's basic interests, will undertake to discover those interests and to place employees in jobs compatible with their existing leanings.

All employees, particularly new employees, need acceptance by fellow workers. When this acceptance is not forthcoming, either through negligence or indifference, the employee feels himself to be an outcast and seeks escape from the unhappy situation. This condition is frequently encountered where there are marked differences of color, race, religion, education, or social status. If the excluded employee does not encounter downright antagonism, he may stick it out until he has won a place in the group, or he may become a loner, or he may quit.

In some of our employee attitude surveys we have asked about the friendliness of fellow employees. In one large company we found affirmative percentages as follows:

Length of service	Affirmative
1 year	40 percent
1 to 4 years	56 percent
5 to 9 years	70 percent
10 to 19 years	81 percent
20 years and over	90 percent

Because most labor turnover occurs during the first few weeks of service, some companies have asked well balanced older employees to serve as sponsors for new employees. A sponsor will take the fledgling under his wing, will introduce him to other employees, eat lunch with him, answer questions and otherwise show him the ropes. A side benefit of this plan is the added sense of worthwhileness it imparts to the sponsor himself. It can be expected that this practice in the future will increase.

Some employees are so maladjusted that they have to be classed as neurotic. They have chips on their shoulders, are overly assertive, withdraw within themselves, feel that the boss has it in for them, seek revenge for fancied slights, take delight in sabotage, defy authority or otherwise exhibit negative traits that interfere with production or morale. In some instances, causes are home problems; even in these situations, job satisfactions can alleviate tensions. It takes a wise and patient supervisor to understand each situation and to provide the milieu which can offset negativism.

Fortunately the percentage of neurotic employees is likely to be small and such employees are easily spotted, for they reveal themselves in aggression, withdrawal or apple polishing and frequently manifest various forms of hate, fear, or guilt. Neurotic employees are easy prey to alcoholism and drug abuse. Many of them fail to realize that they have fallen prey to either of these traps.

A little noted cause of neurotic stress is population density in certain city areas. Much the same occurs in overcrowded departments of a plant, which prevents or disrupts social relationships among employees; sometimes overcrowding causes individuals to block out certain areas which they will defend as "theirs."

Minority employees are frequently a special problem in labor turnover. Real or fancied discrimination against Negro or Spanish-speaking employees undoubtedly causes turmoil and turnover. Personnel specialists assert that cultural deprivations in the childhood of these individuals contribute to irresponsibility, failure to get sufficient education, inability to understand instructions, and a disregard of rules and discipline. Patience and tolerance on the part of those who supervise minority employees are needed.

Female employees constitute an inadequately used source of labor supply. On the average they are better educated than their male fellow-workers. Likewise they usually possess better manual dexterity and seem to be better adjusted to routine tasks than men. They have a higher absentee rate than men, perhaps because of home responsibilities that cannot be avoided. Legislation in recent years has endeavored to prevent discrimination against women, as well as against various minority groups.

In the mid-forties I spoke before the Manufacturers' Association of a large mid-western state. In the December 1943 issue of "American Business," (published by Dartnell) I had an article entitled, "Can We Pay Women Same Wage Rates as Men?" In both talk and magazine article, my theme was that women should be paid the same as men for doing the same work. Criticism from business executives was violent—but their modern counterparts are observing EEO laws, and are not going bankrupt, as had been predicted by 1943 Cassandras!

Absenteeism

Absenteeism is a vexatious problem for most manufacturing companies. In some departments the rate is as high as ten percent on a given working day, particularly on Monday. Absenteeism on Friday will be less if it is pay day!

A large percentage of those who are absent in any given week are repeaters. Alcoholism, drugs, and domestic problems loom large in such cases. Other contributing causes are injury, illness, bad weather, distaste for the task, resentment against the supervisor, labor disputes, sometimes merely a desire to go fishing or hunting, which in itself may be an escape mechanism.

Worker affluence and generous absence policies add to the problem. If a company allows a certain number of days' sick leave per year, employees will consider that it is their right to take this time off, whether they are sick or not.

Underlying much absenteeism is a poor relationship between an employee and his people environment—supervision and fellow workers. Where there is a friendly climate between an employee and his foreman or his fellow workers, there will be less absenteeism, especially if there is conflict in his home life.

It usually pays to concentrate corrective effort on the repeaters. Counseling, medical examinations, job analyses, and foremen collaboration have proved effective in reducing absenteeism of the oft-absent.

Compensation and fringe benefits

We here touch only lightly upon these two subjects, with an eye to the future.

Two trends are indicating need for modifying job evaluation practices. Heretofore job evaluation has been concerned with the content of the job itself—the mental, skill, and physical requirements, the responsibilities and the working conditions. Performance rating of the employee was added to job evaluation to determine whether and when his rate should be increased within the min and max limits established. Two current influences may cause changes of practice:

1. The widespread use of management by objectives (MBO). If specific objectives are achieved by an employee, written performance appraisal may be less needed.

2. Replacing straight-line assembly methods with a series of small production groups may necessitate *group payment* (with or without bonus), to be apportioned among the group members as the members decide among themselves. By extension, this method may embrace plant-wide pay, or incentive bonus, as under the Rucker or Scanlon plans. Moreover, some companies claim success with putting all employees on a salaried basis and not using any form of incentive pay.

Profit sharing and plans by which employees can purchase company stock will probably increase in popularity, sometimes fostered by legislation which prevents high executives from getting these benefits without making them available to all.

Some companies face demands from black employees for their own holidays such as the birthday of Martin Luther King, Jr., and a special day called Black Solidarity Day. Since Gentile and Jewish employees take off special holidays, blacks feel that they are entitled to the same treatment and the same policy as to pay. So far most companies have tried to pretend that this problem does not exist and have passed the buck to foremen to handle it. A management policy will be needed in the future, for it changes the viewpoint from religion to race.

In Europe, and to a growing extent in this country, child-care centers are being set up, sometimes through collaboration of two or more employers. These centers are intended to offset absenteeism caused by working mothers with young children. Along with such centers it is likely that working mothers will want more flexibility as to reporting and quitting times. Already the problems that have arisen include getting competent attendants, compensating them, deciding the age limit of the children who will be accepted and disciplining unruly children.

Companies are discovering that the escalation of fringe benefits is largely a futile exercise; it has little or no effect on morale, absenteeism, or productivity. Employees consider benefits, or additional benefits, as rights to which they are entitled. However, the absence of benefits, or what employees consider inadequacies, can result in considerable grumbling. Fringe benefits can no longer be considered as compensation, motivators, or morale builders.

Tomorrow's actions—NOW

Spend more time, energy and money in improving both original selection, and in internal promotion. Use tests of interest for adjustment to jobs.

Get a physical examination of applicants, to include vision and hearing testing.

Use older employees as "sponsors" for newcomers, but first train them in their duties.

Identify jobs for which there is a shortage in your community and establish protective training programs. Cooperate with local educational facilities for the same ends.

In training, teach the *significance* of tasks as well as the techniques.

Identify, and take firm steps to correct, repeaters in lateness and absenteeism.

Consider day care centers for the children of working mothers in your company.

Help employees who are neurotic, alcoholic, drug users, or otherwise maladjusted.

Maintain a "talent file" of employees, cross indexed as to qualifications and deficiencies.

Remove lower level tasks from highly skilled jobs so that you can get full use of the experience of the encumbents.

Make repeated studies looking toward further mechanization and/or automation.

6

What do we really know about people?

Social Sciences

AN ACCUMULATING body of knowledge in the social sciences is being accepted reluctantly by managers, and is gradually being incorporated into management practice. Economics, which some cynic has defined as the "dismal science," has endeavored for many years to contribute to management knowledge but without much success. Psychologists and sociologists seem to be on the right track. Sometimes it is difficult to distinguish between the two disciplines: psychology is said to be the science of mental processes and behavior; sociology, the study of group or *social* behavior.

Medicine, separately, has developed considerable knowledge about psychosomatics—the relationship between the mind and the body. These interactions can work both ways—emotional states can induce functional, and ultimately, organic disease; physical conditions can in turn affect emotional states. These statements do not preclude ailments caused by bacterial and virus invasions, nor by traumas resulting from accidents or surgical shock. However, research suggests that more than half the hospital beds in the country are occupied by patients who are suffering from physical conditions which *originated* as psychological problems.

Thus job frustration, long endured, can cause heart disease, strokes, stomach ulcers, spastic colons and other very genuine physiological maladies.

Man's daily life is full of stress. All mental and physical effort involves stress. If the athlete wins the race, the artist completes his masterpiece, the salesman makes the sale, the production manager gets the work out, then stress proves to be benign. But if the body is fighting an incurable disease, the company is inexorably going bankrupt or the production manager realizes that he is a failure, then stress is harmful. The conditions which cause harm are twofold:

1. The human being wants something very strongly and after much striving fails to get it, resulting in frustration.

2. He is forced to do something which he decidedly does not want to do.

Under either of these two situations there can be three kinds of reaction:

1. Aggression: the individual attacks, attempts to dominate, resorts to cunning, blames someone else or defends if attacked;

2. Inaction: he attempts to ignore the problem, or defers action in hopes that time will make a decision unnecessary;

3. Flight: he runs away from the problem, substitutes some easier attained goal, or makes himself subservient to someone else.

Any one of these three approaches may be justified in a given situation, but an individual who consistently meets his obstacles in only one of these three ways can be classed as neurotic. Our modern life is so complex that these basic responses may be covered up and surface in a variety of actions and reactions.

The "unholy trinity"

I use the term "unholy trinity" to describe many negative reactions. The unholy trinity is hate, fear and guilt, and they are responsible for most of the unhappiness in the world.

Hate shows itself as attacking, envy, jealousy, playing practical jokes, cruelty, sadism, setting traps, resistance to authority, impatience, intolerance. Fear shows itself as apprehension, indecision, insecurity, timidity, cowardice, "apple-polishing," loneliness, hypochondria and various phobias. Guilt may show itself as a failure to live up to one's self-image; unethical conduct; unjust criticism of others; violation of rules, laws or mores; and attempts to avoid the consequences of current or past misdeeds.

How an individual handles his hates, fears and guilts may determine his emotional maturity. Mature reactions of an individual are usually beneficial to him and to those around him; immature reactions may be harmful to both.

Emotional maturity is likely to be accompanied by equanimity of disposition, adjustment to life, perseverance in the pursuit of objectives, cheerfulness and a prevailing sense of rightness and vibrant well-being. Per contra, immature individuals are likely to be tempestuous, fearful, indecisive, jittery, dejected, hopeless or guilt-ridden. As a consequence they are "out of sorts," depressed or lacking in energy much of the time.

Employee alienation

Employee alienation is one form of maladjustment. Psychologists tell us that the condition results when an employee has a feeling of estrangement between himself and his employing company as to job, working conditions, fellow workers, boss or management practices. He may have a feeling of personal inadequacy as a result of failure in competition with others, deficiencies in schooling, cultural inferiority, inability to perform certain tasks or a lack of advancement.

Because of maladjustments, an employee is likely to believe that the system under which he works is harsh and will not change for his betterment. As in the case of other frustrations, he may take one of the three courses of action cited above:

1. Attack—by rebellion, resistance to authority, destructiveness, careless work or joining a union.

2. Conform—by resignation to his fate, by indifference, or by subservience.

3. Flight—by absenteeism, by quitting his job, by daydreaming or by embracing an outside hobby.

Once an employee has been strongly alienated from his job situation, it is extremely difficult to motivate him. Hence it is important to detect early signs of alienation, particularly in new and young employees.

Previously we have noted that job dissatisfaction can result from failure to satisfy a want or from being forced to do something an individual does not wish to do. By the same token satisfaction can occur from wanting something and achieving it, or from not having any desire for something and not being forced to do it. We can represent the situation by a fourfold table, as follows.

	Action allowed (or forced)	*Action denied (or not forced)*
Strong want	Satisfaction	Strong dissatisfaction
Absence of want	Dissatisfaction	Passive satisfaction

Some studies have shown that dissatisfaction is related to the size of the group. Employees on lonely jobs tend to have more gripes than members of well organized groups. It would seem that an inability to get social satisfactions from friendly contacts results in blind resentment. This finding suggests that the current team approach to production may be quite sound. Related studies have indicated that jobs having varied duties are better liked by employees than jobs that have only one or two minor duties, so supporting job enrichment.

Throughout the day a given employee is subjected to numerous satisfactions and dissatisfactions and the level of contribution he yields to the employer may be the result of these positive and negative forces, many of which are occurring at a subconscious level. Not all positive and negative feelings result from the work situation; the employee may be elated or torn by outside influences.

Characteristics of groups

Sociologists are concerned particularly with the behavior of people in groups. A department is such a group, and it may reveal two kinds of activity; actions designed to get out the production; and actions designed to maintain the solidarity of the group.

Managers think in terms of the first and forget, or do not even realize that the second is ever present. Employees, however, are quite conscious of internal frictions, absence of adequate information, external pressures, freedom of action or its absence, annoying working conditions, inadequacy of materials or equipment provided, etc. Such mundane considerations are quite as likely to occupy the consciousness of employees as are proper facilities for turning out work, work schedules or quality demands.

Groups develop their own norms of behavior, follow natural leaders and tend to discipline non-conformists. As an example, most employees in a shop will accept agreed upon limitations of output even though those limitations might prevent them from earning more money. An employee who refuses to conform and works at a higher pace, so earning higher pay, will incur the wrath of other members of the group.

On the other hand, when there is considerable freedom of choice allowed members of a group, they will frequently set self-imposed standards stiffer than those the boss would have imposed.

> The owner of a small printing plant was offered a large contract but on condition that he turn it out in two weeks. Remembering how often his employees had failed to meet customer deadlines, he was inclined to turn the business down. However, he decided to put it up to the employees in the shop. They themselves set ten days as a deadline and all pitched in to meet it.

Groups are resistant to change much the same as individuals. However, where it appears to be in the interest of the group or to a majority of its members, they themselves can become the instrument of change.

In a western steel company, employees had resisted management attempts to change methods and reduce costs. Part of this resistance had been silent, some of it open opposition through the union. However, when the company and union signed a cost-saving sharing plan that promised large earnings, the union members pitched in with enthusiasm to accept automation and to find other cost cutting devices.

Three theories

Three important contributions of sociologists have altered management thinking: Theory X vs. Theory Y, the hierarchy of needs, and hygiene vs. motivators.

Theory X vs. Theory Y was advanced by Douglas McGregor in his book *The Human Side of Enterprise.* Theory X, he said, postulates that workers are passive, unimaginative, disinterested in their jobs and only greedy for money and security. It considers that workers are lacking in ambition, usually have little sense of responsibility and require strict leadership. Theory Y, according to McGregor, believes that people really want to work, that they will assume responsibility, do creative thinking, be goal directed and exercise self-direction in job performance under proper conditions.

In past years most managers have expressed many of the attitudes McGregor assigned to Theory X. Hence it has proved difficult for practical managers to even consider the implications of Theory Y. Behavioral scientists contend that many of the negative conditions managers face currently have been brought on by their own practices. In addition, outside influences such as better education, more communication, advertising, radio, television, affluence, and different cultural standards have all contributed to make authoritarian methods of managing outmoded. Despite the misgivings of many managers, current trends in management are moving in the direction of McGregor's Theory Y.

The five-level hierarchy of human needs, illustrated in Figure 6, represents the contribution of Dr. Abraham Maslow. Ascending from low to high, these needs are:

1. Physiological—such as water, food, shelter, sex, muscular activity, and bodily comfort.

Figure 6
HIERARCHY OF HUMAN NEEDS
(Maslow theory)

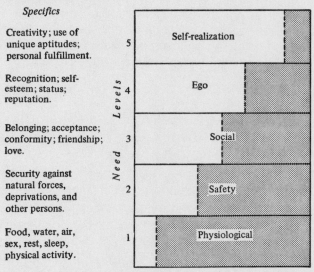

Specifics

Creativity; use of
unique aptitudes;   5   Self-realization
personal fulfillment.

Recognition; self-
esteem; status;   4   Ego
reputation.

Belonging; acceptance;
conformity; friendship; 3   Social
love.

Security against
natural forces,   2   Safety
deprivations, and
other persons.

Food, water, air,   1   Physiological
sex, rest, sleep,
physical activity.

Shaded portion shows estimated percentage of needs satisfied by a typical employee.

2. Safety—protection against physical hazards, threats or job insecurity.

3. Social—acceptance by the group, friendships, love, helping others.

4. Self-esteem—status, recognitions, prestige, personal sense of worthwhileness.

5. Self-actualization—accomplishment, self-fulfilment, opportunity for continued growth and self-expression.

Experience seems to bear out Maslow's belief that needs at a particular level must largely be met before those at the next higher level begin to motivate. As a corollary, a satisfied want is no longer a strong motivator of behavior. Many employers have discovered this condition to their sorrow—they have increased fringe benefits in an endeavor to motivate employees but no added effort resulted.

Our industrial society has largely met the two lowest levels, hence better educated employees are seeking satisfaction in the three highest levels. They may verbalize their groping for satisfactions as a demand for more money, rather than being able to formulate a direct demand for satisfaction of needs in the three higher levels. Actually, the demand for money may be seeking balm for wounded egos, offsets to frustrations, or a means of purchasing satisfiers outside the work situation.

The Maslow theory sees man as a perpetually wanting animal, with a rather small percentage of people achieving the highest levels. Figure 6 endeavors to estimate by the shaded area the percentage of satisfied needs for the average American.

A third important contribution has come from the research of Dr. Frederick Herzberg. One of his conclusions is that the elements which make employees happy in their jobs are not the same elements which make them unhappy. He distinguishes between hygiene, (possible dissatisfier) factors and motivator (or possible satisfier) factors.

According to Herzberg the principal motivators are satisfying work, a feeling of achievement, recognition for good work, personal responsibility, evidence of advancement and personal growth. The hygiene factors are relationships with superiors and fellow employees, working conditions, earnings, fringe benefits, the administration of company policies, status and security. When the hygiene factors are absent workers are dissatisfied; when present, they are merely less dissatisfied. When the motivator factors are present employees tend to be more satisfied in their jobs; when absent they are less satisfied.

Herzberg believes that past scientific management practice is no longer effective; that many of its concepts are outmoded; that the authoritarian way of managing an enterprise is no longer the best way. He suggests that what makes people happy is principally the tasks they perform. Hence he stresses training as a device by which individual workers can do more and better work and hence derive greater satisfaction. He believes that money is a by-product recognition for a job well done and responsibilities properly discharged. He is sometimes referred to as the father of the job enrichment concept.

Another important contributor to sociological knowledge pertaining to people at work has been Dr. Rensis Likert, Director Emeritus of the University of Michigan Institute for Social Research. He believes that driving supervision for higher production or lower costs may lead to a long range reduction in productivity and quality. Under a production-pushing boss, employees feel threatened and become hostile. These attitudes ultimately lead to restriction of production and disciplinary problems. His extensive research over many years showed that the highest producing managers exhibited three traits:

1. Support of subordinates, peers and superiors in the organization.

2. Involvement of subordinate employees in decisions affecting them.

3. The establishment of high performance goals. In connection with the latter, Likert recommends establishing a method of measuring the effectiveness of each work group and, in summary, of an entire company. Included is a feedback system that provides each manager at each level with the measurement results. Using the high-scoring groups as standards, a manager is enabled to determine his own weaknesses and strengths, and to work with his subordinates in the establishment of goals and plans to make his management style more effective.

In summary the work of McGregor, Maslow, Herzberg, Likert, and others suggests that we are failing to utilize the capacities of employees and are in fact using managerial styles that inhibit talents employees have in abundance.

Motivating employees

How to job-enthuse employees who are currently disheartened, disillusioned, and apathetic is a problem that challenges most managers. If there were a simple answer to this question, it would no longer be a problem. We shall here consider some avenues that, in combination, can lead to success.

Motivation is not manipulation; employees are not puppets to be activated by strings developed by psychologists and jiggled by managers. In fact social scientists are the first to decry any such prostitution of their findings. Motivation should benefit both the motivator and his subject, or should result in some important contribution to common welfare in which they both can share.

All behavior is motivated, usually by many forces. Most employees are unaware of these forces, some of which are self-generated wants that surface from time to time; some are outer-imposed by environment, authority or ad hoc necessity. Much routine behavior is self-imposed by employees through a sense of duty or a fear of job loss.

A simple way to understand motivation is to consider that it is the combining of five factors: the sender, the receiver, the climate, objectives, and the message.

These factors are also the principal factors of communication, which is an important part, but not the only part, of motivation.

In industry, the sender is likely to be a manager. By speech, gesture, facial expression, tone of voice, or written communication he transmits information and/or motivation. He expects action to ensue. One-way communication, as in issuing written orders, is weak in that the sender has no way of determining whether the orders were understood and no chance for the recipient either to ask questions or volunteer opinions. Face-to-face communication is two-way, if it offers opportunity for immediate feedback from recipient to sender.

The sender should avoid polysyllabic words or unusual words that may not be known to the receiver, and hence decrease understanding. Use of personal pronouns usually increases effectiveness.

> The story is told of a training instructor who opened his remarks to a group by saying, "If I use any jargon you don't understand, just raise your hand." He then proceeded to explain his subject. At the close of his presentation he asked, "Are there any questions?" One individual raised his hand and asked, "Sir, what does jargon mean?"

True leaders tend to use power words which have emotional overtones rather than to depend solely on logic. They carefully select action verbs or word picture nouns to put over their messages. They accentuate the positive, avoid punishing remarks or sarcasm. They may question results, but not intentions. They work with participants in establishing clear cut goals. Orders, whether written or verbal should be clear cut, should use short sentences, should be transmitted to or through people who understand them and should be given as directly as possible to those who are to carry them out.

Receivers should understand communications and be able to transmit them accurately, or to carry out the desired actions. In any group of employees, differences in intellectual grasp, educational level, vocabulary, or experience are likely to be quite wide. Hence, a manager-sender should evaluate these traits in those he is attempting to motivate. He can often supplement his observations by study of personnel records, aptitude tests, performance ratings, physical examinations, or other data in personnel files.

The specific wants of employees vary because of cultural backgrounds, economic needs, age or self-image expectations. Some employees with low expectations will settle for a low income, provided there is high security; other employees have high ambition and initiative. These opposites will normally not respond to the same motivations or may respond in different ways. An employee's health can affect his receptivity to motivation or his ability to initiate action.

The "climate" under which the motivation is attempted is important. Much of this climate has been created by past relationships. If employees have confidence in a superior, they will be more receptive than if they don't respect him or have definite antagonism toward him. It takes a long time to build a climate of confidence, but it can be destroyed by a single devastating incident.

A superior who criticizes an employee in front of his fellow employees is carrying on communication under the worst possible conditions. In such a situation he is more likely to get negative reaction than desired action. Per contra, conferring recognition in the presence of fellow employees is generally a strong form of motivation. In much the same class are displays of name or photograph under favorable circumstances or the granting of status. Delegated power is a high form of recognition.

We have previously noted that work objectives should be specific and employees should participate in their establishment. Goals which are set too high can ultimately cause frustration, although if the group has participated in goal setting, employees will strive harder than if goals were merely set by the boss. In fact impossible goals dictated by a superior can have exactly the opposite resultant than he expects.

> At one time I worked for an oil company where a district manager said to seven branch managers, "Your quota for the next month is doubled. If any one of you can't make it, I will accept his resignation. The meeting is adjourned." The next day one of the branch managers called the general sales manager at the home office and said, "Jim, I now have 60 percent of the gallonage in my territory. I wish some one would show me how I can double it." To teach the district manager a lesson, the general sales manager ordered him to drop everything else and go to that branch and show the branch manager how his volume of business could be doubled. After a week, the district manager telephoned each of his branch managers to say that of course they realized that he was only joking!

The members of a group will have their individual goals, largely predicated upon their expectations and ambitions. Usually such goals are higher than most will achieve. To the extent that individual goals are consonant with group or company goals, the individual goals will provide self-generated motivating power. Hence it pays a manager to determine the individual expectations of his employees. If they believe that the boss is the one best person able to help achieve group objectives, they will follow his leadership.

The message transmitted in communication should not only be clear as to meaning but should carry some element of motivation. Typically this element is a promise of achievement or reward. Frequently the communication will tell who is to do exactly what, and specify when it is to be completed. Sometimes it challenges the ingenuity of an individual or a group. It should convey the standard by which the efforts will be judged, how progress will be reported to the manager and the feedback to employees themselves.

Above we have mentioned the importance of two-way communication. Actually in an organization of any size there is likely to be, or should be, five-way communication:

1. From a superior down, with feedback to the superior that it is understood and has been carried out. Here is two-way communication.

2. From an employee up, usually in the form of a suggestion or a complaint, with feedback to the employee that the communication has been understood and ultimately what action was taken on it. Here also is two-way communication.

3. Lateral communication from employee to employee, foreman to foreman, or executive to executive.

When all five channels in an organization are clear and utilized, communication is at its best.

> In 1961 President John F. Kennedy ordered the removal of American missiles from Turkey. A year and a half later, at the height of the Cuban missile crisis, Krushchev proposed a withdrawal of Soviet weapons from Cuba if the United States would remove American missiles still in Turkey!

This episode points up two typical management problems:

1. A communication failure to get feedback on orders issued from the top.

2. The inertia of middle managers, many of them selected for conformity, when faced with a change of top management policy.

Corporations as well as governments suffer from the same weaknesses.

Manager actions

The actions of a leader are quite as important as the words he uses, the situation he creates, the standards he applies, the recognitions he awards or the aims he establishes in conjunction with his subordinates.

Actions speak louder than words. Hence a manager who says one thing and does another will soon lose the respect of his employees. Likewise failing to act when action is indicated may have the same result. A superior who attacks a problem vigorously, lives up to his word consistently or administers discipline fairly will soon build a benign climate of confidence between himself and his subordinates.

Here are some specific things that a manager can do:

1. Praise the *work* rather than the worker. This approach lessens the envy of fellow workers and causes the individual to do good work again. Praise of the work should be given in the presence of other employees, so stimulating them to try harder.

2. Call each worker by name at each contact. People are sensitive about names, correct spelling, and correct pronounciation. The controller of a large company once said to me, "The Chairman of the Board has known me for eleven years. So I don't understand why he said to the vice president, 'Get that fat little controller in here.' "

3. Get the opinions of practical workers about situations that affect them.

4. In handling suggestions or complaints listen carefully; rephrase to show that you have understood; delay your decisions to get more facts; give a clearcut decision with reasons for it.

5. Compare the performance of a worker against a standard, not against performance of other workers

6. In using competition, pit group against group, not individual against individual.

7. In handling disputes, be concerned with *what* is right rather than *who*.

8. In meting out discipline, your actions should be fair, firm and consistent; "the punishment should fit the crime."

9. If you have to criticize, do so as to methods or results but rarely as to motives. Conduct the interview in private, with questions, not with accusations or belittling remarks. Sometimes it is useful to find two minor points to praise, one at the beginning and one at the end of each session, with the "meat" sandwiched between.

10. Hold each worker responsible for previously agreed upon *results*.

Communication lies at the very heart of motivation. Where it is lacking, an organization will be static. With good communication and galvanizing motivation, an organization can become dynamic.

There are problems of communication other than between management and employees. Communication with suppliers, customers, stockholders, and with the public in general are separate problems that require careful analysis and planning.

Production by teams

If it is true that our present organization of business fails to utilize the latent talents of many employees, then there emerges a new role for supervisors. In the past they have been taskmasters to drive employees to get out to work. In the future they can become coaches, coordinators and consultants, to help employee groups get out the work.

In many companies extreme subdivision of labor (as on the assembly line), time study standards, motion economy, production scheduling, standard practice instructions and similar management techniques have depersonalized some tasks to the point where employees can no longer derive satisfaction from their tasks. We have previously pointed out that these conditions may result in loafing, day dreaming, restriction of output, avoidance of responsibility, emphasis on security rather than on personal growth—accompanied by demands for more money so that satisfactions can be bought on the outside.

Many types of production lend themselves to the team approach. This is particularly true where the total production consists of sub-units or sub-assemblies that are readily identifiable. The classic example is the automobile. Companies like Volvo and Saab have successfully turned over much production to semi-autonomous groups who make many internal decisions for themselves, rotate their members for versatility of experience and have a considerable say in division of earnings.

The team approach becomes a new challenge for top management as well as for the immediate foreman. Obviously the efforts of groups must be coordinated as to total output and time. Lagging groups must be supported. Conflicting groups must have their conflicts resolved. Some one at a high level must allocate space. Procurement of raw materials and semi-finished parts cannot be left to the individual teams themselves.

Experience shows that such teams tend to elevate their own leaders who may have no special title but who will provide an internal motivating force different from that which comes from an appointed foreman. Many foremen are puzzled or resentful at this new organization form, believing that it takes away their authority and changes them into staff consultants rather than line supervisors. Other foremen are happy to be put in the role of the team coach, and find less necessity to assert authority. This new type of organization frequently has the effect of bringing foremen into more direct contact with the production effort. Instead of always solving problems that arise, they serve as moderators of group meetings where the employees undertake to work out their own solutions. Instead of just handing out production quotas a foreman discusses with his group what quotas can be met, and passes this information upward.

Within a group, employees rotate various jobs so that they get added experience; the net effect is job enlargement. Research psychologists suggest that such enlargement increases the ability of each employee to fulfill his own potential through acceptance of responsibility, meeting challenge and the joy of achievement.

A number of questions about this new form of organization remain unsolved. One, for example, is whether the group should be permitted to interview and approve new members much as the foreman has done in the past, or to get rid of inefficient or uncongenial members. Job training can largely be handled by the members of the group itself, but compensation becomes a problem many groups are unable to solve. We have previously pointed out that job evaluation may in the future be concerned with evaluation of earnings for all jobs in a production team, rather than for the job of each individual. The fair division of the earnings of such a group remains an unsolved problem.

Motivating middle managers

Much has been said about the importance of motivating rank and file employees; rather little about middle management. In the past foreman and middle managers were expected to have a single-minded conformity to standard operating procedures. Management looked askance at middle managers who wanted to depart from the way things had always been done in the past. In recent decades, top executives have felt the turbulent winds of social change blowing inexorably on the barren desert of management tradition. Their response has been to attempt change through new top management policies, only to discover that middle management people were squatting comfortably in their own little deserts of tradition. This discovery has brought out a need for motivating middle managers.

For such individuals, more money and job titles do not seem to be as effective as they have been in the past. The best motivators seem to be recognitions for accomplishment, challenge, participation in management decisions, job enrichment, and manager development to qualify encumbents for higher jobs. In the realm of financial return, profit sharing, stock options, and deferred compensation are preferred over cash bonuses by higher paid managers; foremen and low-level middle managers, many of whom have given up hope of ever going higher, generally say with Omar Khayyam, "Take the cash and let the credit go, nor heed the rumble of a distant drum."

The chief executives of many companies face a corporation generation gap. Young managers seem less willing to work their way up than they used to be; many want either instant success or are disinterested in further promotions. At the same time the average age of managers is decreasing as more young people come into managerial posts. In fact many large corporations follow a policy that if an individual has not shown, by the age of thirty, that he has considerable potential, they will pass him up as a candidate for a future high-level job. By the same token, an individual who is earmarked for development and promotion finds himself strongly motivated to learn more, to do more, to accept more responsibility and challenge. Since all available signs point to a stringent shortage of managerial talent in the decade ahead, present top managers need to locate and develop managerial potential, if management succession is to be generated internally.

A little understood and little used motivation at all levels of our society, is the role played by expectation. Children will strive to meet the expectations of their parents; however, if those expectations are too great, then frustration of the child may result. The worker who accomplishes a difficult task set by his foreman basks in the rewarding glow of his own sense of worthwhileness. A production worker once said to me, "I did more than I thought I could because my boss said I could."

We are only beginning to understand the value of managerial expectations for individual and group performance. The concept is the heart of management-by-objectives. Employee performance and career progress are definitely related to the goals which have been established, and particularly if key employees have had a part in the goal-setting process. Most of us tend to do only what we believe we are expected to do; rather few of us set higher goals.

The value of high expectations is particularly great in hiring college graduates. Normally these individuals are placed under an old line foreman who may have subconscious envy of his subordinates, may have no concept as to their ability or any plan to bring out the best in the young people assigned to him. As a consequence the new college hire may settle on lower standards than he is really capable of meeting, so impairing his own self-image and leading to negative attitudes toward his job, his boss and perhaps toward a career in business. Either foremen should be taught how to set difficult goals for college graduates under them or those graduates should report to some higher level executive who understands the motivating power of such expectations. High performance normally takes place in a framework of expectation. Low challenge yields low performance by employees, college trainees, or managers.

Tomorrow's actions—NOW

Critically examine your own written and verbal communications with others; also your actions as a leader.

List what non-financial incentives you personally provide to subordinates and others.

List what non-financial incentives your company provides for middle managers; identify middle managers who are worthy of promotion.

Set high, but not impossible, expectations for employees, but individualized for their respective abilities.

At least once a year, review the personnel records of employees who work for you, and of those with whom you have frequent contact.

At least once a year, attend a seminar on worker psychology, sociology, motivation, or similar subject.

Read the writings of Douglas McGregor, Abraham Maslow, Frederick Herzberg, and Rensis Likert.

Identify employee examples of hate, fear and guilt (the unholy trinity). Seek ways to alleviate their maladjustments.

Study possible applications of job enrichment, and probable resultants, pro and con.

Consider the possible benefits and risks in the formation of production teams, with payment of group bonuses.

7

Unions: The other kind of conglomerates?

How unionism has evolved

THE HISTORY of unionism in the United States has been a stormy one. It is not a new movement; there were trade unions shortly after the American Revolution that established the rates of pay for which their members would agree to work. This unilateral practice in turn led to collective bargaining, originally for wages, hours, and working conditions.

Around the middle of the 19th century the Industrial Revolution took hold in the United States. It was characterized by increasing concentrations of wealth and the development of the factory system of production, which soon gave rise to a number of craft unions. In the 1870s and '80s the Knights of Labor flourished. This movement attempted to unite all workers into one organization, regardless of the type of work performed. The organization had a meteoric rise and fall, yielding to the craft unions, which in 1886 united as the American Federation of Labor.

The Congress of Industrial Organization (CIO) had its genesis as a section of the American Federation of Labor, but became an independent union in 1936. Instead of being organized by crafts, it was organized by companies and industries, taking all employees in a given company into one local. It was largely aimed at mass production industries such as steel or oils. After a number of abortive attempts to combine these two big union organizations, they were successfully merged in 1955, comprising about ten million workers from the AFL unions and five million from CIO unions.

Not all large unions are members of the AFL-CIO combination but it is so representative that most individuals consider its actions as indicative of organized labor in general. The contracts AFL-CIO secures for its members largely set the demand-standards for smaller unions.

It is estimated that about 28 percent of people at work are members of some organized union. The six largest unions are Teamsters, Auto Workers, Steel Workers, Machinists, Electrical Workers, and Carpenters.

Labor legislation

Labor legislation over many decades has been of two general types, protective laws and labor relations laws.

Protective laws, both federal and state, have covered child labor, safety, conditions of work for female employees, workmen's compensation, occupational disease, minimum wages, hours of work, and other factors relating to the worker, principally in an industrial environment.

Labor laws have largely pertained to the relationships between employers and employees, particularly employees in organized unions. These laws have covered the right of employees to organize, unfair practices by both employers and unions, collective bargaining, governmental mediation, arbitration, injunctions, handling of employee funds by either employers or unions, and the conduct of labor disputes.

These matters have been covered in a succession of labor laws, mostly federal, of which the following can be considered the most important:

1. The Railway Labor Act of 1926;
2. The Federal Anti-Injunction Act of 1932 (Norris-LaGuardia Act);
3. The National Labor Relations Act of 1935 (Wagner-Connery Act);

4. The Labor-Management Relations Act of 1947 (Taft-Hartley Act);

5. The Labor-Management Recording and Disclosure Act of 1959 (the Landrum-Griffin Act);

6. The Civil Rights Act of 1964 (Anti-discrimination by race, color, religion, sex, or national origin);

7. The Occupational Safety and Health Act (OSHA) 1972; and

8. The Pension Reform Bill 1974.

In addition to the above milestone labor legislation there have been other federal laws aimed at inequities in employer-employee relations. Since federal laws apply only to inter-state commerce, many states have passed enabling laws to make many of the same features of federal legislation applicable to the states for intrastate employers.

In retrospect it appears that much of the early labor legislation was designed to prevent employer exploitation of labor, but more recent legislation has tended to curb the power of organized labor. Throughout, there has been a marked tendency for federal and state goverments to set themselves up as mediators of labor disputes or as arbitrators to decide labor disputes. Unions tend to resist arbitration because they feel that they have sufficient power to force employers to do what they wish; employers tend to resist arbitration because they feel that most of the awards of arbitrators favor unions. The outlook is that public opinion will force more arbitration, or possibly legislation to set up industrial relations courts to make binding decisions.

Since the turn of the century consumer prices and unionized labor costs (including fringes) per unit of output have pretty much varied in unison. It has been a leapfrog process with first one then the other going ahead. In this spiraling process, members of large and belligerent organized labor unions have made out better than members of other unions and decidedly better than unorganized workers who indirectly help pay the higher rates of union members. Since possibly 70 percent of ultimate prices can be traced back to labor costs, it must be evident that wage increases that exceed productivity contribute to cost-push inflation.

It would be unfair to lay all the blame for inflation on the cupidity of organized labor. However it seems apparent that inflation will not ease until we create better ways to handle worker wage problems, possibly by industrial relations courts that will utilize job evaluation techniques on a national scale. In a later chapter we shall see that other contributing factors such as price gouging by employers, government overspending, and mismanagement of fiscal and monetary affairs add fuel to the flames of inflation.

The power of organized labor

In recent decades organized labor's clout, often supported by laws, has made collective bargaining a farcical procedure. The strike, or strike-threat, has caused many employers to capitulate rather than to bargain; higher prices were an easier choice than a closed plant.

Higher living standards for all our people result mainly from additional capital investment in tools and equipment; organized labor, through socially sanctioned coercion, has annually taken a disproportionate slice of the technology-generated larger pie, leaving the rest of the pie to be divided among unorganized workers.

Some recent demands by organized labor have included:

1. Wage increases;
2. Cost-of-living clauses;
3. The right to refuse overtime work,
4. Retirement after 30 years of service, regardless of age;
5. Large severance pay for layoffs caused by technological change;
6. Profit sharing;
7. A voice in management decisions as to sending work to outside contractors, making changes of working methods, closing a plant, etc.;
8. The right to renegotiate labor contracts under certain conditions;
9. Changes in working procedures to reduce drudgery and monotony; this demand seems to be a belated union acceptance of job enrichment;
10. More education for employees. The intent of this de-

mand is to make it a subject for collective bargaining, not an action to be decided by management alone.

White collar unions

White collar employees are joining unions in record numbers and these unions are increasingly winning representation elections. Teachers, nurses, hospital employees, clerical employees, technical and supervisory employees, all of whom have witnessed their buying power eroded by inflation, are joining white collar unions in great numbers. Part of this condition results from the wage success of organized blue collar workers. Moreover the myth that white collar jobs are secure jobs has been exploded in many situations.

Even professional people such as engineers, lawyers and to a less extent doctors and dentists are setting up professional associations which more and more act like unions in speaking for their members and even in calling strikes. The move is worldwide and not confined to the United States.

A survey of 3,000 middle managers conducted by the American Management Association, revealed that nearly half of them favored laws requiring bargaining through managers' unions and that more than one-third said they would consider joining such a union. Many said that they resent being left out of important decisions and the lack of authority commensurate with responsibility.

We shall have a brouhaha society indeed if someday the American Bankers Association, the American Medical Association, the Sales and Marketing Executives, the American Management Association, and similar nationwide groups decide that they will paralyze the whole country, which they could readily do with strikes. Should this kind of thing ever occur, democracy will be dead.

In recent decades we have witnessed municipal, state, and federal employees forming unions and staging strikes. In some situations leaders of goverment have capitulated to excessive demands for wage and retirement benefits. The result may be such a heavy burden on taxpayers and people at work that some governmental units will collapse.

The repercussions of strikes reach far beyond the employers—and decrease total productivity in the dreary process. People are getting tired of a succession of strikes of various groups, which tie up whole communities or whole industries and actually are blackmail against society. For example, maintenance mechanics of an airline can prevent the airplanes from flying, causing hardships to thousands of passengers. Utility employees on strike can darken an entire community and deny service to millions of people. Truckers on strike can almost starve a city and cause the loss of millions of dollars in wasted food. Striking teachers deny education to children. Striking garbage collectors affect the health of a city. Striking firemen and policemen prevent security to citizens who have already paid for it. As a result, free collective bargaining (which never was free) is slowly yielding to enforced arbitration, a trend which moves us in the direction of a socialized state.

Costs of strikes

Our barbaric system of strikes deals heavy blows to the economy. The costs include:

1. Profit losses suffered by the struck company;
2. Related losses to suppliers and to sales outlets;
3. Losses to whole communities in business failures, taxes, real estate values, property damage, accidents, expansion of industry, church contributions, charity, etc.;
4. Loss of total production to the whole economy;
5. Losses to the employees on strike, including family health; and
6. Losses in earnings are frequently not made up in increases wrested from employers.

Over recent decades the number of man-days idle due to labor-management disputes has increased year to year. Currently, it equals the production of 50,000 people working for a full year. In union relationships we still live under the law of the jungle.

It has been my first-hand observation that most strikes are caused by a small percentage of bellicose dissidents; the inert majority does not want to strike but "goes going" with those who do.

Taxpayers subsidize strikes

Taxpayers largely subsidize strikes. Four kinds of government and other public funds added to union benefits, mean that many employees can earn almost as much when on strike as while working.

The public funds which frequently support strikers are:

1. Welfare payments;

2. Unemployment compensation, moneys for which come largely from employers, which then can be used against them. In many states workers can qualify for these benefits if they merely refuse to cross a picket liine;

3. Food stamps; and

4. Aid from United Fund Charities.

Such use of public funds depletes the funds themselves, reduces total productivity, results in longer strikes, yields inflationary wage settlements, increases taxes, causes disruption of communities, and invites workers in other companies to follow suit. Vote-seeking politicians are largely responsible for this uneconomic situation.

Inflation has resulted in an ever increasing number of cost-of-living clauses in union contracts. Typically such clauses call for wage increases of one cent per hour for each 0.4 percentage increase in the Labor Department's consumer price index. Most such adjustments are on an annual basis; some are quarterly. They are in addition to increases negotiated through collective bargaining.

Large wage settlements and cost-of-living escalation clauses must fuel the cost-push inflation spiral, unless productivity increases are offsetting, which rarely is the case. If all union members ultimately get cost-of-living protection, it will in essence be paid by the three out of four workers who do not belong to unions, plus people on fixed incomes.

On the brighter side there is mounting evidence that the strike is becoming obsolete as a union weapon. This situation is a paradox of affluence. When workers were earning sixty

cents an hour, they had little to lose by striking. However the earning power of *skilled* workers is now so high that they can scarcely hope to continue their modes of living on strike and welfare benefits, which may however be adequate for the semi-skilled and the unskilled. George Meany, president of AFL-CIO, himself has said, "Strikes of people getting $7,500 or more a year just don't make sense." Leaders of the United Steel Workers, noting that in the face of threatened strikes, steel users have stockpiled overseas supplies or substitute materials, have concluded that the strike is becoming less useful to organized labor. The net effect of these views on the part of labor leaders may be to make collective bargaining a more constructive force than it has been in the past.

Our nation surely deserves a better fate than to allow any organized group to climb on the shoulders of all other groups, whether organized or not. The time is ripe for a much-to-be-desired collaboration between management and union leaders.

It is not to be expected that organized labor will ever surrender the concept of collective bargaining. However in past decades, collective bargaining in the United States has revolved around how much the employer would give, rather than a quid pro quo. In the words of one employer, "I bargain and the employees collect." In England more than a million workers operate under a productivity bargaining agreement; under this agreement employee benefits are granted in return for changes in work practices or conditions that are calculated to lead to high efficiency. In addition the two parties agree to joint objectives. Although no one would cite the English situation as ideal in employer employee relationships, nevertheless this particular kind of productivity bargaining seems indicated for our future.

Donnelly Mirrors, Inc., of Holland, Michigan, provides an example of productivity bargaining as part of successful participative management. An employees' committee decides on a percentage increase to be requested and presents the figure to management. Translated into dollars, the total is increased by approximately 50 percent to determine the amount of cost savings required to justify the payroll increase. Richard N. Arthur, Senior Vice President, states that the company's experience reveals that savings have rather consistently *exceeded* the required savings.

In the United States as management by objectives takes hold, some of those objectives are bound to be introduced into bargaining sessions. This would seem to be a healthful sign.

In England, after World War II a practice originated in unions which was known as "working to rule." It represented a meticulous adherence to all the rules under which employees operate. The net effect is a slowdown but instead of losing earnings, as during a strike, employees receive regular earnings. Airport controllers and railway employees have used this delaying tactic to win wage increases and other benefits usually sought by means of a strike. A little noted by-product of the practice is that it tends to give employees guilt feelings, because they know they are doing something that hurts the interests of their employing company and they know that they are not working to capacity. The practice has not taken much hold in the United States, although it has at times been used.

In recent years a new word has come into the lexicon of economists: stagflation. It means a relatively stagnant period while at the same time inflation occurs. It is likely to be accompanied by some unemployment. When business is booming, employee demands for wages and fringe benefits can readily be added to the cost of a product; when business is falling off sharply, employees and their leaders usually temper their demands. But in a period of stagflation, employees find their earnings buying less and less because of rising prices. However employers find inventories building up because of decreased demand, even though what demand does exist is willing to pay a higher price.

Management of unions

Unions, too, face a management problem, partially resulting from bigness. The United Auto Workers, with 1.5 million members, the United Steelworkers, with a million members, and the International Brotherhood of Teamsters, claiming two million members, are huge conglomerates, holding labor contracts in a great variety of industries. They have payroll, accounting, investment, legal, personnel, and administrative problems not greatly dissimilar from those of large corporations. Their executives are well paid—the presidents of many large unions earn $100,000. per year or better, between salary and expense accounts.

Forty-seven unions in the U.S. have more than 100,000 members. Their leaders cannot keep close touch with rank and file members. As a result rebellion is on the increase.

Factionalism also presents problems: skilled vs. unskilled; white vs. black; the young and better educated vs. older members with less education. These various mixes require that negotiators must win something-for-everyone contracts.

Traditionally, unions have pressed for job seniority in deciding which employees should be laid off and rehired. Some court rulings are suggesting that this practice may be illegal if low seniority could be traced to past hiring bias against minority employees and females. Both past practice and court rulings ignore the importance of experience and work performance; i.e., merit.

In recent years, social objectives have been on many unions' shopping list: anti-pollution, insurance of members, greater protection against job and industry hazards, cost-of-living escalation for retirees, civil rights, equal opportunities, and joint management-labor action in layoffs. Unions are also demanding a voice in awards to contractors, plant closings, overseas plants, and contemplated mergers. Some of these demands arise from growing economic and social sophistication on the part of union leaders and their staff advisers.

As well managed unions accept social responsibilities they would do well to tell the general public about it. Unions, as well as industry, get some bad publicity in the press, which finds negative issues more newsworthy than positive actions.

The merger movement has hit unionism, partly as a result of joint bargaining sessions and partly as an offset to the power of corporate conglomerates. However, such mergers tend to destroy the homogeneity of a union, putting added pressure on officers and negotiators.

Young union members particularly reveal an interest in improving the quality of life as well as in increased earning power. The younger leaders of many unions have never encountered the strife faced by a former generation. Their claims are broader than the traditional "wages, hours, and working conditions." They express doubts about the seniority system, about the appointive powers and integrity of some powerful top union leaders. They opt for greater social progress.

Union members are asking more questions, rejecting agreements negotiated by their leaders, repudiating crooked leaders, and in general are injecting into the union movement a rambunctious dynamism it hasn't felt for some decades.

Future confrontations between giant corporations and powerful unions could bring about titanic struggles that may be resolved only by new laws, compulsory arbitration, or industrial relations courts.

Social progress could be greatly accelerated by a triumvirate of management, union, and goverment working jointly toward common goals. There are hopeful signs that each of them is coming to a recognition of the potential contributions of the other two. It is idealistic to believe that such a partnership will come to pass through voluntary action of the three parties—but the insistent pressure of international competition may do what rationality has failed to do.

Future of labor-management relations

The future of employee relations seems to hold out these possibilities:

1. A continuation of past trends, likely resulting in compulsory arbitration of disputes or in industrial relations courts that will have the same effect.

2. Federal and/or state laws that will prohibit work stoppages under certain conditions and substitute mediation or arbitration with fact-finding by an elected or appointed con-

tinuing panel. This alternative may adopt many of the practices already in effect in the public sector, since 30 states have such laws applicable to public employees.

3. More realistic collective bargaining, wherein each party gives up something in exchange for something granted by the other party. In such a climate, the things granted and given up should all contribute to improved productivity.

4. Improved handling of grievances.

5. Labor and management cooperating for higher levels of production.

Number four above is already in effect in many companies. One of the best examples is found in the steel industry where the labor contract between the United Steelworkers and the ten largest steel makers includes an "expedited arbitration" procedure. In the past, a year or so went by before an employee's grievance could be heard and settled. Under the new procedure certain types of routine grievance are handled at the first or second step of the previous five-step grievance system. The new method provides for an informal meeting of the complaining employee, his union representative, and his immediate supervisor. In the past an employee had to file a formal grievance to get a hearing. Expedited handling of grievances in the steel industry now totals less than ten percent of costs under the old system. Arbitrators are required to issue decisions within 48 hours after a hearing.

Many companies have a relatively simple system of handling minor grievance cases, but in large companies the procedure has become so complex as to become both unwieldly and costly.

For an example of better collective bargaining, consider General Electric Company, which over many years has been plagued with strikes, one of which lasted more than 100 days. At one time it had a policy of making a firm offer prior to labor negotiation, then sticking with it through thick and thin. As a result, labor contract negotiations were marked by bitterness and strife. The company had to deal with more than a dozen different unions including two large ones—the International Union of Electrical Workers and the United

Electrical Workers. In the new setup, both sides meet from time to time during the life of a contract to iron out any problems in its administration. This improved communication sets up an atmosphere under which reasonable leaders of both sides can discuss problems without acrimony. Both management and union feel that a new day has arrived in labor negotiations.

Other examples of the interdependence of management and employees are found in the Kaiser Steel Corporation of California, Goodyear and Goodrich Tire Companies in Akron, Ohio, and the Chicago and Northwestern Railway.

Practical considerations frequently enter in. In the case of the Kaiser Steel Company, Japanese competition was about to force the closing of the plant. The two Akron rubber plants were so old that they had difficulty competing with newer plants elsewhere in the country. Changes in working rules made it possible for the Chicago Northwestern Railway to get business it otherwise would not have. The steel and electrical industries have both suffered from foreign competition. When antagonists face a common enemy, they find that they can pull together.

West Germany has "codetermination" in large industries, a system that provides worker participation in management decisions. It is credited with giving West Germany the best record by far among industrialized nations as to lost working days per 1,000 employees. Employers, however, believe that the legislative-backed practice endangers property rights, keeps foreign capital from setting up German operations and will gradually cause a flight of German capital away from industrial production or out of the country entirely.

No one expects Utopia in employee-employer relationships but it does seem that there is growing understanding on both parties that they must work together for the common good rather than against each other for mutual harm.

Tomorrow's action—NOW

Prepare and maintain a chart that shows your average employee earnings and the cost of living in your area since 1960.

Study and improve the grievance handling procedure in your company.

Go into grievance or collective bargaining sessions with carefully prepared documentation in support of your position.

If you negotiate with unions, study their history, leadership, past actions, organization, etc.

Before you engage in collective bargaining with a union, learn all you can about quid pro quo "productivity bargaining."

In strikes or labor strife, take your case to the people in your community. Aloof silence rarely wins public support.

Set up a communication procedure with labor leaders (or with employee representatives if you have no union) that functions throughout the year.

Familiarize yourself with legislation dealing with union—employer relations, and keep up to date on changes.

part three

The new look of business functions

8

Production—men, money, and materials

Types of production

IN GENERAL, manufacturing methods fall into three classifications, unique, mass production, and process.

Unique production turns out goods made to a customer's specification, as in a jobbing machine shop. Or, it may produce small job lots, as in furniture manufacturing, where a certain design of chair may be produced in quantity. Again it may be batch production, as in a newly organized chemical company which manufactures a single product. Unique production is characteristic of small companies. However some small companies produce one or two items in large quantities, for which they purchase special purpose machinery or introduce straight-line production, thus moving toward mass production methods.

Some numerical (tape) control equipment, usually limited to mass production, can be applied to unique production if the tape control makes possible certain variations of product and if volume justifies the large investment required. In other words there is no sharp line of demarcation between unique production and mass production. A company may at one and the same time be mass producing certain items

109

while other items are made to customer specifications or are produced in small job lots.

Characteristic of unique production is likely to be that all manufacturing is done in one or two plant locations, although marketing may cover a wide area.

Whereas unique production was initiated in the United States in the middle of the last century and was the first manifestation of the industrial revolution, mass production has been a phenomenon of the present century, aided by mass transportation, advertising media and mass markets.

Characteristics of mass production are high volume; relatively few variations of product; use of mechanical and/or automated equipment; and integrated planning, scheduling, and control of production.

Peter F. Drucker in his book, *The Practice of Management*, differentiates two types of mass production—the production of uniform products and that which "manufactures uniform parts but assembles them into diversified products."

Much mass assembly is handled by what is termed straight line, or assembly line, production. It is made possible by considerable sub-division of labor and conveyor systems with other materials' handling equipment: unloading devices, fork lift trucks, pallets, driverless tractors, storage systems, standardized containers, fixed or mobile cranes, overhead monorail systems, and fixed or movable roller or bulk conveyors.

In unique production, work is likely to be taken to various machines for processing; in some situations, as for example in manufacturing large vats or heavy boilers, workers may bring their tools to the work. In straight line production, standardized products (or standardized parts for later assembly) are manufactured by moving the work through a predetermined sequence of operations, typically using some kind of conveyor system.

Considerations that lead to setting up production lines are:

1. Work-in-process has to wait extended periods; or the cost of moving it from machine to machine is high

2. Considerable machine hour cost is involved in set-up, or in idle time of production equipment

3. Labor hours can be reduced by straight line production; the company already suffers from labor shortages

4. There is volume demand for the products of such a production line

5. Products or parts can be manufactured to stock, without unduly increasing inventory costs

6. Quality can be improved

7. Cheaper or more durable materials can be utilized

8. Floor space can be conserved

9. Operations now performed in distant departments can be brought to one production line

10. Supervisory attention and time can be reduced

Against these considerations must be viewed the current blue collar blues, thought to emanate from the boredom of doing small portions of the total production job along an assembly line. If job enrichment for work done on an assembly line is undertaken, the balancing of enlarged tasks becomes difficult. Some companies are reporting success with forming small worker teams for sub-assemblies, so capturing some of the values of the assembly line technique but also getting the benefits of team effort.

The term automation is loosely used to mean a number of recent developments, some of which are mere outgrowths of past mechanization and some of which are new developments made possible by applications of electronics and electronic data processing to manufacturing operations. In the early use of the word automation, it tended to mean development of special purpose machinery. Later it embraced tape control of production machinery and processes. Still later it came to embrace the idea of computer control of manufacturing.

Automation

In its fullest meaning, automation integrates automated equipment into continuous production, with feedback that can adjust processes to improve quality. Involved are servo-mechanisms that can start, stop, increase pressure, record temperatures, or otherwise alter mechanical operations. If these operations are tied to a computer, the feedback information can be processed by that computer for reporting to management or for activating the servo-mechanisms.

In an automatic production line, there can be automatic loading and unloading devices, transfer between machines, automatic gauging or inspection, feedback yielding automatic adjustments, in-process storage units, automatic assembly, packaging, and conveyorization away from the last machine on the line. Sometimes the production line is a *dis*assembly line, as in a meat packing plant where the whole animal is reduced to a number of final products.

The application of the electronic computer to production is of course only one of its many uses. Other uses will be discussed in later chapters.

In manufacturing, the computer is finding and will find additional applications in planning, operations, and controls. Fundamental are various data collection systems or networks. Typically there are source data-recording terminals at various points in the plant. The data are recorded by means of keyboards, dials, pre-punched tabulating cards, badges, or tickets. Such entries usually record job numbers, time and work completion. Some data entry devices offer limited inquiry possibilities. When information is transmitted electrically to a computer, the computer can store or process the information and at appropriate times print out the results. As an example of output, manufacturing costs can be produced to show labor, material, and manufacturing overhead, as well as variances from standard costs or budgets.

We have already seen that the computer can also be used to control manufacturing processes. In this application, work-procedure programs are stored for various machines or processes and fed out to them as needed. The procedure includes feedback information with adjustments ordered by the computer when input data exceed allowable limits. This type of feedback usually does not require human intervention and, as is the case with source entry information, can be stored, processed, or summarized.

The future will undoubtedly see utilization of time-sharing

computers, not located on the premises of a company, being used to control remote manufacturing processes.

The computer can be used as an excellent coordinator, reordering parts when inventory becomes low, revealing ill-balance in supplies for production, showing up potential idleness or overloading of machines, compiling man-hour needs, giving early warning of failure to meet customer deadlines, etc.

Process manufacturing

So far we have discussed unique production and mass production. The third type is process manufacturing, typified by the oil and chemical industries. Early activities in these industries required much manual labor. With the advent of servo-mechanisms and computer controls, labor costs have been sharply reduced.

Servo-mechanisms in process industries can control temperature, viscosity, rate of flow, color, acidity or alkalinity, specific gravity, and other attributes of liquids or gases. If standards for these attributes are programmed into a computer, the computer can direct the servo-mechanisms to take the necessary readings or the necessary actions to control the process from beginning to end. The classic example is a refinery that operates at night with one man. He is a night watchman!

Many servo-mechanisms contain three elements: a sensing device, an amplifier, and an electric motor or hydraulic piston, which typically opens or shuts valves.

It is difficult and costly to apply servo-mechanisms and computer control to existing process systems. It is far better to devise and design those systems around the automatic features from the very outset.

Utilities can scarcely be classed under the three headings we have outlined above for manufacturing. It is true that gas and electric companies produce something measurable. Railroads, other transportation companies, telephone, and other communication companies provide services. Legislation has long since recognized them as utilities, granting them monopoly in the areas they serve. Their activities and equipment differ considerably from the manufacturing processes that turn out a tangible product. Nevertheless their management problems have a great deal in common with those of manufacturing enterprises.

Four problem areas in manufacturing

An overview of the manufacturing problems which top management faces reveals four large areas: the need for capital investment to supply production equipment; planning, operation, and control of the manufacturing processes; personnel problems; and foreign competition.

Most companies engage in some kind of formal or informal long range planning. Typically these plans cover marketing, manufacturing, finance, research and development, diversification, acquisitions, and personnel. In most companies an important section of such planning deals with plant and equipment for manufacturing. This portion of the long range plan must be integrated with other portions, all of which will take into account forecasts as to the economy, political environment, sociological demands, technological improvements, and competition.

Long range planning for utilities is their most important management problem. Planners must peer far into the future, long term investment commitments must be made, and huge capital sums must be raised.

There is a scarcity of highly trained individuals skilled in the techniques of long range planning.

In recent decades, considerable progress has been made in calculating return on investment (ROI). Three types of calculation are frequently found: the current return on present investment, the expected return on proposed new investment, and the difference between a proposed investment and alternate uses of the money.

Some of the best material on proposed investment in machinery and equipment has been published by the Machinery and Allied Products Institute of Washington, D.C. Its "Business Investment Manual" is a comprehensive classic on the art of investment analysis.

Many companies are leasing industrial equipment instead of purchasing it. Some advantages are:

1. The practice conserves working capital
2. Rentals are deductible before tax
3. It avoids equity financing, which is frequently difficult to get and which furthermore dilutes ownership
4. It avoids the fixed interest on indebtedness (bonds, mortgages, debentures), which in times of business recession might impose undue burdens. Moreover, lenders of large long-term funds frequently impose restrictions on management as to payment of dividends, executive salaries, or other actions.
5. Leasing may decrease taxes that would have been paid on owned assets.
6. Leasing may give a company access to large credit sources that might otherwise be unavailable.
7. Leasing may prove to be a hedge against obsolescence of equipment in an industry with rapid changing technology.
8. In some instances the lessor will maintain the equipment, so saving maintenance costs to the lessee.

While these advantages seem great, they must be measured against other considerations. One is the rate of depreciation on owned equipment, allowed by the Internal Revenue Service. Another is the body of stipulations in the leasing contract. A third is the undeniable fact that the leasing company must make a profit from the transaction, a profit which has to come from the lessee.

Some companies have found it expedient to sell large equipment or even an entire plant to a leasing company, and then to lease back the equipment or plant for continuing operation.

As is the case with return on investment, leasing of large equipment is a complicated subject, not one for amateurs. Hence there is great opportunity for you, the reader, if you wish to specialize in this subject. It requires knowledge of accounting, taxes, depreciation, contract law, corporation finance, and the pertinent mathematics. Many accountants believe they are competent in this general area without knowing what they do not know.

Managing production

At the heart of production management lies skillful planning, close scheduling, coordinated operations, inventory management, and overall production control. These five factors in turn must themselves be carefully coordinated. In some companies, as much as one-third of the assets represent inventory or work-in-process. Economists have long since pointed out that rising inventories of all industry, along with decreasing utilization of manufacturing capacity, foretell economic recessions, even when sales for a time seem to hold up at a reasonable level.

Production planning establishes the level of manufacturing activity for a given period of time. In light of actual operations, it may require frequent revision. The main factors that enter into production planning are orders on hand; forecasts of sales; the expected availability of labor, raw materials, equipment and storage space; and the demand for funds these factors create. Scheduling assigns due dates for completion of customer orders or for production that will be added to inventory. Inventory control attempts to maintain a balance between manufacturing supply and customer demand; it must take into account the lead-time necessary to replenish various types of inventory. Additionally it must be sensitive to the ups and downs of the business cycle.

Production *control* must serve two functions:

1. To insure that production planning is carried out; however, feedback from internal operations and from external economic forces may cause it to serve a second function:

2. To modify the planning to keep it in better balance with sales and sales forecasts.

The future of this area of production management will undoubtedly revolve around the application of advanced mathematical procedures. It will take into account such concepts as lead-time in manufacturing, inventory costs, accounting concepts (such as LIFO or FIFO), formulae for economic lots, nomographs for determining the relationships among three variables, reorder points, supplier lead times, inventory turnover, investment in inventory, probability mathematics, and inventory writeoffs. Most companies are naive as to these computations and use simple indices such as inventory turnover, in an attempt to solve a much more complex problem. Hence great opportunity exists for those individuals who will qualify themselves for intensive research in these important areas.

Industrial engineering

Industrial engineering is a broad term which embraces layout, flow of work, time study, motion economy, process engineering, etc. In some companies it includes production control, quality inspection, costs, machine design and other related activities. Its principles have been successfully applied to office and sales work and even to the operation of a large electronic data processing department!

Many books on industrial engineering are available to you if you are interested in finding a career in this field. Also many colleges offer night courses in various aspects of it; some colleges have four year courses which lead to an IE degree, or its equivalent. These courses include advanced mathematics (statistics, linear programming, game theory, simulation, etc.) and utilization of the electronic computer in problem solving.

In past years the industrial engineer has accented production economies, and this accent seems destined to continue.

However, any manufacturing foreman or manager can effect work simplification in his domain by use of the procedure detailed below. I have found that the method can readily be taught to employees, so getting their voluntary involvement in seeking economies.

The plan is called STEM-analysis because it seeks cost reductions in Space, Time, Energy, and Materials.

Each of these factors is investigated as suggested in the following outline:

STEM-analysis procedure

Factor and sub-division	Typical analysis
Space	
One dimension	Analyze flow of work
Two dimensions	Review floor layout
Three dimensions	Consider more shelves, storage space, elevators, pallets, and fork lifts
Time	
Waiting	Study work in process, congestion, unnecessary stops, or storage
Traveling	What other methods for moving work through the production cycle?
Production	In what ways can productive work be simplified or eliminated?
Energy	
Human	What physical work could be done by machines?
Mechanical	Where could more mechanical power be used? Or gravity?
Electrical	Consider electric power, automation, feedback, communication, lighting, and electronic applications
Materials	
Raw	Specifications, purchasing, inspection, substitution
Tools	Specialized tools, jigs, fixtures
Equipment	Auxiliary or new; maintenance; return on investment

STEM-analysis does not approach the sophistication of industrial engineering techniques. Nevertheless, it will stir employee imagination and sometimes cause them to ask for more scientific studies of certain operations.

As a very young man, I was privileged to attend a luncheon tendered to Harrington Emerson, a renowned management engineer and author of a management best seller, *The Twelve Principles of Efficiency*. Sitting at the head of a long table, the aging Emerson said, "In my life, I have earned several million dollars, and I am going to tell you how I did it." He paused, looked around the group and continued, "I have looked at present working methods and persistently asked, 'Why?' Usually, the end result was a better *How.*"

Personnel problems

The personnel problems of *production* management are probably the most complex of all personnel problems in business and industry. Since these problems are considered in many chapters of this book, we shall here merely mention that they rather readily fall into such categories as selection, training, compensation, fringe benefits, research, union relationships, and supervision. The frequently mentioned "blue collar blues" are thought to be more prevalent among employees in manufacturing than in other functions, especially where line assembly methods prevail.

Mechanization and in more recent years automation, have given rise to another problem: the layoff or transfer of displaced workers. Frequently this subject becomes important in collective bargaining agreements and may involve guarantees against job or income loss, severance pay, early retirement benefits, job security provisions, grievances, guarantees of income for employees moved into lower paying jobs, retraining, seniority rights, preferential rehiring after layoff, moving expense allowances, advance notice of coming layoffs, and joint labor-management committees for handling other situations arising from employee displacements.

As a result of loss of defense business, the Riverside, California, plant of Alcan Aluminum Corporation had to cut its force from 1,200 to 600 employees. To overcome disrupted morale, management established "operation speakeasy." Under this plan, employees signed up in groups of three to have lunch in the cafeteria with a senior manager. In these small discussion groups, employees asked questions, or volunteered opinions; ultimately 80 percent of all employees participated. The principal topics discussed were productivity and ways to improve it, 32 percent; causes of low morale, 26 percent; poor communications, 23 percent; and work environment, 18 percent.

The company issued bulletins, stating actions to be taken,

explaining certain situations or giving reasons why suggested actions were not practical. Both morale and productivity rose. Since the plan was designed to offset the chaotic conditions resulting from a drastic reduction in workforce, it did not become a continuing personnel program. J.N. Smith, director of industrial relations, says, "Such a program should be used to solve a specific problem, be limited to a . . . stated period of time, and not be repeated for several years. . . ."

The future should provide opportunities for specialists skilled in solving the labor problems that result from technology and automation. Such a specialist will need to combine the knowledge of an economist; the experience of a personnel manager; an understanding of foreign competition; and comprehension of a changing technology, including automation and computers. To these attributes he will need to add the wisdom of a Solomon.

Foreign competition

Rank-and-file employees are largely unaware of the effects of foreign competition, until it hits a whole industry as it has in the textile, camera, radio, television, steel, and shipbuilding industries. Nor do employees realize that wage increases, not offset by increases in production, can price American goods out of foreign markets, invite a flood of lower priced imports, or cause employers to set up plants in foreign countries.

Labor leaders are quite aware of these situations. For the most part they have sought Federal umbrellas as answers, rather than increased productivity of union members.

Managers should bring the facts of foreign competition home to their employees. One company prepared an exhibit of its own products against competitive foreign products, with price tags attached to both. The disparities in selling prices were practical lessons in economics, which were not lost on employees.

In a later chapter we shall consider "productivity bargaining" with union representatives. If this practice becomes widespread, it may ease the problem of low cost foreign competition and reduce the pressure of cost-push inflation.

The decade ahead may be one of social disquietude, but production will be needed world-wide to meet the demands of expanding populations and expectations. There is no doubt that future manufacturing offers lucrative managerial opportunities if you are willing to prepare for them.

Tomorrow's actions—NOW

Since manufacturing usually presents the most difficult personnel problems, keep abreast of trends and new developments in personnel practices by joining the American Management Association or a similar organization.

Master the pros and cons of group incentive pay plans.

Determine which of your products lend themselves to more advanced mass production methods, such as assembly line, special purpose equipment, tape control, and cost control centers.

If handling of heavy or bulky materials is involved in your production, get surveys by conveyor manufacturers, but have them evaluated by experienced consultants.

Update production planning and control with special emphasis on recent mathematical and graphic procedures.

Get competent and unbiased counsel on applications of the electronic computer to your manufacturing operations, with cost and savings estimates. This advice holds true for production, process or utility companies.

Master the techniques for calculating return on investment in large capital equipment. Contrast ROI with leasing costs.

Apply a breakeven chart to make-or-buy decisions in the production department.

Study modular containerization, and its influence on transportation and materials handling equipment, with sealed containers outside-coded for electronic scanning as to contents and destination.

9

The huckster's wagon

Selling throughout the ages

MODERN salesmanship has an ancient, but not always honorable, heritage. For many centuries the barter system prevailed for exchanging goods and services. Later, the use of gold or silver in bulk or coins simplified trading; still later, paper currency issued by stable governments eliminated the necessity of carrying heavy coins. Today checks, credit cards, and accounting entries make unnecessary even the exchange of much paper money.

In the Middle Ages, merchants were a relatively low class of society. However as they prospered, many of them became wealthy and capable of lending large sums to governments, princes, and to would-be military conquerors. Many became wealthy landowners or traders, who did business with other countries through ownership of sailing vessels.

The Industrial Revolution which began in England in the late 1700s, rapidly spread to other countries on the continent. It did not really take hold in the United States for another 50 or 75 years. Up to the middle of the last century, our economy was basically one of agriculture. However over the last half of that century, production became of increasing importance. Salesmen of manufacturers traveled from town to town or from state to state, offering their wares. The

122

"traveling salesman" bore an unsavory reputation and became the butt of many jokes. The medicine man bottled crude oil or other concoctions and offered them as panaceas for man's many ailments.

Some companies placed their wares in horsedrawn wagons and drove from town to town or from farm to farm. Fruits and vegetables were often sold in this way and the drivers of these wagons became known as "hucksters." Later the word was used in a derogatory sense to apply to over-imaginative advertising copy writers.

In the first quarter of the present century, companies had sales departments but these were normally considered adjuncts to the all-powerful production departments. World War I in 1918 and World War II in 1941 gave powerful impetus to mass production. Over this same period transportation and communication improved radically, making mass consumption possible. The sales department of many companies became as important as the manufacturing department. However it was still the objective of most companies to sell what they could make; it was not until recent decades that the concept of making whatever could be sold was accepted, leading to product diversification, massive mergers, and conglomerates.

Sales management is concerned principally with the product or service being offered, and with the operation of a sales force. It is a narrower concept than marketing management, which will be considered in the next chapter.

Analysis of the product or service should identify the end utility. Here are a number of products or services together with suggested end utilities:

Product or service	Seeming utility	Possible end utility
Automobile	Transportation	Social acceptance
Bicycle	Health	Companionship
Hair dye	Appearance	Retail job
Watch	Tell time	Impress friends
Accounting course	Job in accounting	Business for self
Mink coat	Keep warm	Status symbol
Country club membership	Play golf	Business contacts

The above illustrate that the ostensible purpose of a product or service may not be its end utility. The automobile salesman who says to a prospect, "Wait until your friends see you whizzing by in this swanky job" is appealing to the end utility, but if he says "This car will give you twenty miles per gallon," he is appealing only to an intermediate and uninspiring utility.

End utilities for consumer products are likely to be personal satisfactions; for industrial products, they are likely to be higher productivity, reduced costs, or better quality. A sale becomes a good sale when it converts a customer into a friend of your company.

Selecting salesmen

The problem of managing a sales force falls logically into the following four sub-divisions: selection, training, compensation, and supervision.

Selection of salesmen is one of the most difficult types of selection management faces. The salesman is confronted not only with understanding the product or service, but also adjusting to the territory or to the circumstance under which selling occurs and to the needs of the prospect. Technical information or demonstrations may be involved. Some selling work requires that the salesman be away from his family for days at a time.

There are vast differences among retail, wholesale and industrial selling; within each of these classifications there are wide variations. In most retail selling the prospect comes to the salesman; in wholesale and industrial selling the reverse is generally true.

For most companies the following program of selection will prove useful:

1. Prepare job analyses of the different kinds of sales work. Such analyses should include a clear statement of duties and the conditions under which the job must be performed; the educational or mental requirements; personal skills needed; physical effort; responsibilities and authorities. The very act of preparing specifications of this nature may partially indicate the type of applicant needed.

2. For applicants who claim experience, tests can be developed. These may be tests of product knowledge, practices in the industry, end utilities, etc. For applicants who do not claim experience in the particular kind of sales work, tests of intelligence and interest may be indicated. In using such tests, a sales manager should bear in mind the Supreme Court ruling that selection tests must be "job related." This means that a company might be called upon to prove that applicants who did well in the tests became better salesmen than those who did poorly. The psychologist uses the word validity to indicate this relationship; in installing new tests, a sales manager should employ a psychologist who not only can set up the tests but also prove their validity.

3. The application blank, and the information asked of applicants in an interview, can provide the interviewer with very useful data. Some companies, after careful research, have been able to assign points credit, or demerits, to data on the application blank—age, kind, and amount of education and experience, height-weight ratio, hobbies, etc. Scores under this plan predict the chances of success.

Government regulations prohibit asking race, color, national origin, religion, and to a certain extent sex or age. Discrimination against applicants because of these attributes is forbidden by law. If a salesmanager rejects an applicant for any one of these factors, he must be prepared to defend his action, if questioned. Some of them are obvious in an interview, even though they may not be asked on an application form. Most companies have a personnel manager who is well informed as to government regulations and the sales manager will do well to consult with him before setting up an application blank for sales applicants.

4. Sources of labor supply for the sales force can become important. A salesman who has been selling services, for example, may be a poor candidate for selling hard goods or technical equipment. Many companies find that present employees provide excellent sales trainees, especially for selling and servicing technical equipment. Interest tests used in employment can frequently uncover present employees with sales potential. Order clerks likewise may yearn to be out on the firing line.

Many years ago, research by the Sales Executives Club of New York concluded that the average labor turnover cost for a wholesale salesman was about $8,800. Today this figure must surely be 50 percent higher. Hence it pays to open up many sources for locating sales ability or potential.

Training salesmen

Training given new salesmen is important. Many companies provide excellent training as to demonstration or information about product or equipment but inadequate training as to prospect needs, end utility or sales presentation. Some sales jobs are little more than order taking; others require great persuasion. In order taking it is important that the salesman know all details shown in his catalog or sales promotion book; price, discounts, shipping information, delivery dates, etc. In persuasion, he needs additionally to understand prospect needs, arouse interest, show satisfaction from end utilities, answer objections, and convince the prospect to the point of signing the order.

The persuading salesman needs to sprinkle his presentation with *power words*. These words are distinct from the ordinary in that they carry emotional overtones as in the following examples:

	Ordinary word	*Power word*
Verbs	shines	glamorizes
	wants	yearns
	says	proclaims
	works	drudges
Nouns	dirt	muck
	dummy	blockhead
	feeling	passion
	cell	dungeon
Adjectives	pretty	radiant
	strong	everlasting
	critical	acrimonious
	dangerous	death-dealing
Adverbs	angrily	spitefully
	well	superbly
	easily	gently
	quickly	instantly

There are power phrases of use to a salesman—similes and what I call "pedastal" words. Here are some examples:

Similes

   Hard as armor plate

   Shiny as the colonel's boots

   Colorful as a florist's window

   Soft as milkweed down

Pedastal phrases

   A man of your standing

   I need your help

   Your long experience

   Because of their respect for you

Flattery and insincerity are soon detected by sales prospects, so a salesman must find some genuine trait to mention. However, most people are hungry for recognition of even minor attributes or accomplishments. Properly used, power words, similes and pedastal phrases can open channels of communication between a salesman and his prospect and at the same time give the prospect a pleasurable emotional experience.

Carefully phrased questions can help the salesman understand a prospect's true needs, his objections or alternate considerations for use of his money. This kind of information is particularly valuable to the salesman when the economy is less ebullient than in past years.

Sales training is, or should be, a continuing process. Changes of product or of policy necessitate some retraining of the present sales force. The efficient use of a salesman's time, getting information in advance on prospects, the proper coverage of territories, servicing of customers, and locating new prospects are parts of sales planning that can be taught to both new and old salesmen. In some sales training situations, the use of programmed instruction and other visual aids can be both informative and stimulating.

Compensation

The problem of compensating salesmen seems to be one that is never settled with any finality. Many companies change their pay plans every few years, only to discover flaws or to encounter criticism, leading to further revisions. Any company that endeavors to keep all salesmen happy with its compensation plan is chasing an elusive will-o-the-wisp. It is wiser to develop a plan that moves the maximum amount of goods with minimum sales expense, and to seek salesmen who will accept or adjust to the compensation plan in effect.

In a sales force of any size, the top quarter of salesmen will normally account for fifty percent or more of the dollar sales volume. Per contra, the bottom quarter of the sales force may account for a small percentage of total volume, much of it sold at little or no profit. Sometimes this negative resultant is caused by an incompetent salesman, sometimes by a poor territory, and occasionally by bad judgment of sales management. Whatever the cause, it deserves analysis and corrective steps.

As is well known, there are three major types of sales compensation, straight salary, straight commission, and salary or drawing account plus some form of bonus.

The base salaries for various kinds of selling, or for various territories, can be determined by job evaluation methods. Salary alone offers little monetary incentive to a salesman to produce a greater volume.

Some salesmen or independent sales representatives prefer a commission basis. In fact some manufacturers' agents, wholesale distributors and jobbers, in business for themselves, earn far more than if they were on the company payroll as a salesman. One value of the commission basis is that the sales cost per unit is fixed and an individual's earnings are determined by how hard and effectively he works. From the standpoint of a manufacturer this situation may provide a limitation because some commission agents may be independently wealthy, or constitutionally lazy and hence fail to exploit the potential of territories assigned to them.

Many sales managers hope to set up a salary-plus-bonus plan that will give security to the salesman and at the same time offer sufficient incentive to increase sales volume. Typically such a plan will provide two-thirds of a man's total income as base salary with opportunity for an additional third in incentive earnings. Variations in such plans are great; no one has yet found a formula universally acceptable, or applicable within a given industry, or successful during both upswings and downswings of the business cycle.

Some managers offer contests with prizes; some distinguish achievement by status symbols such as size of car; others attempt to enlist the support of the wives of salesmen through alluring premiums offers.

Surveys have revealed that in any given year about the same number of companies will be changing to salary plus greater incentive as are switching back to plans with larger salary base. Over a long period of time, it would appear that the salary base for salesmen (*i.e.,* security) is increasing as the latitude for incentive pay decreases.

A recent trend on the part of some manufacturers is to undertake direct selling to eliminate middlemen; or to buy out distributors to make them part of the company's marketing organization. Since distributors frequently handle competitive lines, part of the motivation for the last practice is to eliminate competition in a given territory.

Supervision

The supervision of territory salesmen is a difficult aspect of sales management. Some managers make it a practice to ride territories with salesmen from time to time, thereby hoping to determine how well a salesman knows his territory and what reaction he is getting from his distributors and dealers. This practice can be an effective, albeit sporadic, kind of supervision.

Another method is by the establishment of carefully prepared quotas. Prior to the beginning of each year, each salesman is asked to indicate what dollar sales he anticipates from each customer, classified by products. He also estimates the number of calls he expects to make on present customers, and the number of prospects he expects to convert to customers. These data are broken up into monthly or sometimes weekly figures and later the actual calls and sales are compared with the salesman's original estimates.

Other companies require a salesman to prepare a weekly

plan, which he submits to the home office and against which his actual calls and sales are compared. In situations where salesmen or manufacturers' representatives are paid purely on a commission basis it becomes difficult to force them to do any such planning, or to correct them if the home office does not like the kind of planning submitted. It is also true that even where salesmen are paid on a salary basis, sometimes the "star" salesman refuses to be bound by such paperwork.

The sales manager

We are here considering the salesmanager as a supervisor of salesmen. Sometimes he reports to a vice president; more often he is top man in marketing. Usually he will spend at least one quarter of his time in the field riding territories, meeting important customers, making analyses of opportunities or studying competition. He must be alert to changing demand and recommend changes of product or service accordingly. If the company has a market research unit, he will keep in close touch with its findings. He uses territorial quotas as control and may in addition operate a sales budget. He is responsible for the hiring, training, compensating, transfer, and promotion of salesmen. He is an active boss, capable of closing or helping salesmen close important deals.

Either the sales or marketing manager will want to forecast future sales predicated on past performance. Raw data of monthly sales over a long period (ten years or more) can be analyzed to determine a long-term trend of growth or recession; cyclical variations above or below the long-term trend; and seasonal fluctuations, by months, within a calendar year.

Extrapolation of the trend, with cycle superimposed, can lead to annual forecasts, which in turn can be fractionated into monthly expectations.

A competent market researcher will master the statistical techniques involved in this kind of forecasting.

The most successful salesman or sales manager is one who puts himself in the shoes of the prospective buyer. Hence he may analyze the problem which a potential dealer-customer faces and show a solution to that problem based on company products or services. To do this he must understand the customer's problems and preferably have contacts at various levels of the customer's organization: his shop, purchasing and engineering departments, and top executives. His sales work becomes a process and not an act. His role is more like a consultant who has been brought in as part of the customer's team. His success may depend, not so much on how many calls he can make per month, but rather on how well he solves the problems of his potential customers.

There was a time when a successful sales manager was one who could corral lots of sales dollars. It was up to somebody else in his company to worry about profits. That time has passed. The sales manager must understand the profit margins of various products, how much service he can afford to give in connection with those products, which customers are profitable, which prospects are worth pursuing, and which demands of the market are increasing or decreasing. He is a profit minded-businessman, not merely a supervisor of salesmen.

A study by the Sales Manpower Foundation of New York determined that the average tenure of sales managers was only 4.6 years. The principal reason for failure was that "he's poor at analyzing data."

A very large portion of sales management deals with sales personnel problems, many of them mentioned in this chapter. Most are unique to sales work. Hence, the future may offer real opportunity to you to steep yourself in the specialized procedures used in sales selection, training, compensation, and supervision. These activities provide large stepping stones to higher jobs in sales work.

If you are in selling, or if you look forward to a selling career, let me shock you with a direct quotation from Lawrence A. Appley, now chairman of the board of the American Management Associations and for many years its distinguished president. In a letter to me he wrote, "There is now and will be . . . a great demand for good marketers. There hasn't been any real honest-to-God selling in this country for 30 years." I take this statement to mean that the affluence of three decades has made the hard sell largely unnecessary—but the current outlook is quite different!

At the retail selling level, there are startling innovations. Automation is finding applications in department stores and food chains. IBM, Sperry Rand, National Cash Register, and others have developed point-of-sale systems which scan coded marks on packages to record price; use tickets for entry data into computer terminals; provide instant validation of a customer's credit; pick up merchandise information by passing a "wand reader" over bar-coded tags or labels; transmit data to a central computer, which overnight prepares reports on sales, credit, inventory, tax, etc. Other retail innovations have passed the experimental stage.

Store managers who are versed in electronic applications to retail merchandising will be needed in increasing numbers; the equipment manufacturers are prepared to train you for such a career.

Opportunity in sales management? You'd better believe it!

Tomorrow's actions—NOW

As a sales manager, use *validated* employment tests in selecting sales personnel. Use more women and minority employees in sales jobs.

Use audio-visual aids in developing salesmen by filling in gaps of knowledge, experience, attitudes, or selling practices.

Ride territories with salesmen to note their sales approaches, their acceptance, and their deficiencies.

Develop sales contests, promotion plans, and premium offers.

Organize sales conventions for serious work, not merely play.

Analyze the sales force: appraisal of results, reasons for failures, revisions of compensation plan.

Compensate salesmen for profitability, not merely for sales volume.

Include salesmen in product planning, quotas, market strategy, and policies.

Work with schools to improve the image of selling as a career and to have courses in selling included in the curricula.

Pay close attention to sales expense, budgets, profitable items, territory planning, and control.

Estimate the remaining length of life of your principal products.

List all unique strategies used in the past by your sales competitors; plan counter strategies.

Revise selling policies and practices to improve dealer and consumer confidence in the company and its products.

Where feasible, eliminate middlemen in the distribution of your products.

10

King consumer still sits on his throne

Marketing management

MARKETING management is a larger concept than sales management. The difference is also one of point of view, for selling basically expresses the needs of the producer to convert his products into cash; marketing is interested in discovering and satisfying the needs of consumers. Mass production puts a premium upon selling, for the goods must be moved away from the factory into the hands of buyers and consumers. Mass marketing has become possible because of increased density of population centers, mass transportation, and improved communication. Mass production has fostered mass marketing and vice versa.

Marketing management looks at the big picture. It is customer-oriented rather than product oriented, is constantly on the alert for opportunities to create products and services that will satisfy customer needs. Failure of management to heed customer needs has brought about the downfall of many industries. The classic example of course is the railroads; their managers thought of themselves as operating railroads, whereas customer needs were for door-to-door delivery such as could be supplied by trucks, or faster trans-

134

portation such as could be supplied by airplanes. The motion picture industry supplies another example: its management saw its role as producing motion pictures but television managers thought of themselves as supplying home entertainment.

Many companies feel secure if their product is one needed by an expanding, affluent population. However they may be lulled into a false sense of security because of competitive or substitute products, which may be cheaper or more adapted to consumer needs.

The oil industry provides an example of an adaptive industry. Originally crude oil was regarded as a medicine with many applications. By the time this theory was exploded, the industry was refining oil for lamps of the world. With the invention of the incandescent light bulb, this use faded rapidly. Petroleum next was converted largely to gasoline for the internal combustion engine and to fuel for heating of homes. Later oil was converted into gas, petro-chemicals, and became a constituent part of many plastics. Oddly enough some of the uses for petroleum were developed outside the industry and should not be credited to management shrewdness of that industry.

The electronics industry offers a current example of product orientation. Managements in this industry are top heavy with scientists and engineers. They favor research, development, and production; marketing is an afterthought. At the outset, the effort in the computer field was to develop large capacity, sophisticated equipment, and this effort continues. Little thought was paid to the possibilities of small computers and the needs of small companies; it took several decades before these demands were met. Had companies in the early years been market oriented, they would have uncovered a thousand uses for small and relatively inexpensive computer and communication equipment.

Modern marketing management is concerned with market research, consumer research, product innovation, sales planning and control, servicing and distribution facilities. In essence it works back from consumer needs through production to raw materials. Its viewpoint is that a company is or should be a *customer satisfying* entity, not merely a goods producing one. Consumer research is a part of, but not co-extensive with, market research.

The American Marketing Association has adopted the following definition: "Marketing research is the systematic gathering, recording, and analyzing of data about problems relating to the marketing of goods and services." In general three distinct methods have been developed:

1. The statistical method utilizes historical data within the company or industry; available economic data from governmental or private sources; and projections of population, buying power, competitive products, international trade, etc.

In studying the national picture, market researchers need to take advantage of input-output analysis developed by W. Leontief. This method relates the product inputs (from other industries) required for each given industry to the output of that industry. The concept is useful in large scale planning.

2. Market sampling usually is done by personal interviews, either of potential consumers or of knowledgable distributors and retailers. If these samples have been scientifically selected, the findings have considerable applicability to the whole market being surveyed. In some situations experiments can be set up under controlled conditions. For example, two territories may be contrasted as to results from different products, different packaging, different sales appeals or distribution methods, etc. Again, direct mail and retail outlets may be contrasted as to volume and costs; or the results from company wholesale salesmen may be pitted against results from use of manufacturer representatives.

3. Consumer research is interested not only in consumer needs as to products or services but also as to attitudes and motivations. For example, a prospective automobile buyer may state to an interviewer that his need is for a small simple car to provide him transportation, but his innermost motivation may really be for a swanky status-symbol car. Consumer research is more intimate than overall market research, for it is concerned with what satisfactions people are seeking, how they believe certain products or services will meet their

needs, how they compare various brands, how important is price and what attitudes they hold toward various companies.

The simplest form of consumer research uses mailed out standard questionnaires, sometimes offering a low cost premium for a reply. Or, questionnaires can be put in the hands of relatively inexperienced interviewers who elicit the answers by personal interview. Sometimes highly experienced interviewers do in-depth interviews with selected samples of prospects. In the case of the latter method, indirect approaches may be used in order to draw conclusions as to subconscious motivations. If consumer and motivation research interest you, you can find considerable literature on these subjects in any large public library.

Psychologists sometimes use a projective technique with volunteer subjects who may answer questions, such as word association responses or sentence completion. The stimuli used are generally designed to get information about a given product, service, or company, which in turn must be interpreted as to its significance.

Sometimes a need surfaces without any research at all.

> A young woman, an avid "soap opera" watcher, noted that many of her friends wanted to learn about episodes they had missed. She started a newsletter covering 14 serials, soon found she had a profitable business. Here is an example of a woman who saw a need, and devised a service to meet it.

Considerable research suggests that the buying needs of people in different cultural levels vary considerably. Beer at one level may give way to whiskey at another level or to fancy wine at still a third. Trends in the field of consumer research suggest that real opportunities lie ahead for those trained in psychology, sociology, motivation research, communication, and statistical analysis.

Product innovation

Most companies believe that the development of new products is essential to survival. They point to the fact that in the case of most successful companies large percentages of sales volume result from products not in existence 10 or 15 years earlier. These products are the survivors; only the companies themselves can tell of the disasters that resulted from launching many past products. One researcher told me that in his long experience, eight out of ten new consumer products had failed to gain market acceptance.

Many companies find that older products become subjected to increasing competition or to lessened demand. As the profitability of such products drops into the red, companies are reluctant to remove them from the line until or unless other products can be introduced that will fill the gap of sales volume needed to accept the spread of sales overhead. Some companies believe that it is necessary to retain loss items so that they can offer a full line; as a consequence, the profitability of the selling effort is an averaging of loss items against profit items.

In some companies the suggestion of a new product is the result of a brainstorm by a major executive. In this instance a lot of people may "jump on the bandwagon" without adequate market research to determine whether the proposed product has a good chance to succeed.

> At one time our organization was asked to audit the work of a research and development department in a medium sized paper company. The manager of the department was very proud of the fact that he had 11 projects under way. A careful analysis of these projects indicated that only two of them could be sufficiently profitable to warrant further research. We recommended that four be put on the back-burner for possible future development if market conditions improved and that the remaining five should be abandoned.

Some companies have numerous suggestions for new products, and these products should be evaluated. In this situation it is desirable to form a new product rating committee that will include the sales manager, advertising manager, market research head, controller, manufacturing manager, head of the research laboratory, etc.

For a given product this committee sets up ten pertinent

criteria on which the suggestion will be judged, such as probable manufacturing cost, need for new personnel, probable length of time to develop, competition, capital required, etc. Each committee member then records on a scale of one to ten, his judgment as to each of the ten criteria, after which their respective ratings are compared. Frequently this comparison results in lively discussion. Frequently, too, it results in prompt abandonment of the proposed bright idea, so saving the costs that might otherwise have been involved in laboratory effort.

If a proposed product has received high marks in the first screening, it should be subjected to a more intensive scrutiny. The committee may wish to discuss additional items like the following:

1. The market—ultimate users; their location; potential dollar volume; must demand be created; existing competition; advertising and selling problems.

2. Reasons for developing the product—to be competitive; to get additional sales volume; for greater utilization of company resources; to take advantage of present by-products; to use specialized knowledge or skill of certain employees; to reduce costs.

3. Effects on production—new capital needed for equipment or research; building or storage space required; personnel needed; procurement problems; and estimated costs.

4. Effect on marketing—need for market or consumer research; use of present sales force; distribution channels; cost accounting to determine genuine profitability; additional marketing expense; desirability of utilizing test markets.

If consideration of a product passes this second screening, it can then safely be turned over to the R & D Department for practical development or for pilot plant production of enough units to be tried out in test markets.

New products can be killed by setting a high price intended to recoup quickly research and development expenditures, without regard for what the consumer proves willing to pay; or by failure to coordinate advertising, sales promotion and sales effort; or by lack of patience in winning consumer acceptance. Since new products suffer such a high infant mortality rate, anyone skilled in keeping more "babies" alive will find an eager demand for his services.

Importance of service

Because many products are tangible and much service is intangible, the importance of servicing is often overlooked.

> In the early stages of the computer, one large typewriter company developed an excellent large computer. However very few of them were sold because, unlike its huge competitor, the company did not have servicing facilities scattered around the country. Its computer venture became a financial disaster.

Most automobile manufacturers are product-oriented and depend on dealers to provide service; the result has been many unhappy automobile owners. In most industries of the future, service jobs and product servicing will become increasingly important.

Marketing managers more closely resemble the company controller than a salesman, for they are likely to be dealing with market statistics and cost reports, rather than with the techniques of selling. Their expertise is greatly needed in long range company planning. Through quotas, budgeting, costs, sales analyses, and computer printouts they exercise control over the sales manager and the selling effort. They may have to determine the proper size of a territory as outlined below. In the future marketing management will, like sales management, offer a rewarding career.

My longtime friend, Al Seares, retired vice president of marketing for Remington Rand and twice president of the Sales and Marketing Executives International, has suggested two valuable concepts to add to this book:

1. The U.S. Bureau of the Census should calculate the "value added by marketing" as a useful fraction of the "value added by manufacturing" computation. I agree with him that it could be a useful index.

2. Marketing is so important to the success of most companies that they should endeavor in their respective commu-

nities to reach young people in high school and college to point out career opportunities. SMEI has a useful program in this direction, in which Al Seares is taking an active part.

Distribution channels

Consumer goods can be sold through many distribution channels. There can be direct sales by means of mail or company retail outlets. There can be several types of wholesale distributors who will maintain a limited stock and in turn sell to retailers; some manufacturers sell directly to retailers, chain stores, discount houses, or mail order houses. Some companies use manufacturers' representatives instead of having their own sales force, particularly in sparsely settled areas where selling expense would be high. Some companies sell through brokers who do not handle the goods at all but merely transmit orders.

Many companies have a mixture of different distribution methods. They will have their own sales force to call on wholesalers or large retailers; will use manufacturers' representatives who may handle other lines; will accept orders by mail or from brokers; will sell directly to industrial users, although this practice is not prevalent in the case of consumer goods but is standard procedure in selling industrial equipment and materials.

Repeated analysis is needed to determine whether channels of distribution should be changed. Some "middle men" cause high final prices, which limit sales volume, or they reduce gross profit over what it could be in situations where direct selling would be warranted.

For you there may be a future as a wholesale distributor or manufacturer's representative. Alternately you may become a sales or marketing manager who must study the economics of the company's distribution system.

Determining size of a territory

Territories are typically too large for intensive cultivation, which means that many salesmen just skim the surface. Yet those same men will fiercely resist any attempt to cut territory size.

A marketing manager can block out the proper size of each territory by considering:

1. The present and prospective customers—their location, purchase potential, and credit rating.

2. The number of *genuine* sales calls a salesman can make in a week, and the number of hours he works.

3. Geography of the territory—size, terrain, density of outlets, roads, and transportation facilities.

4. Competition.

5. Profitability; percentage of sales expense.

Customers and prospects should first be classified—as in the example shown below, with each classification defined in advance—in collaboration with the territory salesman:

	Territory calls		
Classi-fication	Calls per year	Customers plus prospects	Total calls
A	50	6	300
B	25	24	600
C	12	52	624
D	4	80	320
E	2	120	240
			2,084

If a salesman can reasonably make 30 calls per week (1,500 per year) it becomes evident that this territory is either too big for one salesman, the call rate must be scaled down or the classifications revised.

By checking weekly sales reports the marketing manager can determine whether calls are being made as planned and whether actual sales are justifying the A to E classifications. Dollar sales quotas can readily be added to this procedure.

Since so few companies have any analytic method to determine territory size, there is obvious opportunity for you in this type of work, if you have an interest in statistical research. The need exists.

Sources of information

Market research is either lacking, or is poorly developed, in most companies, yet there already exist numerous sources of valuable information, such as those listed below:

Federal government, Washington, D.C.
Bureau of the Census publications: manufacturers, housing, agriculture, population; consumer income, farm income, personal income; *Statistical Abstract of the U.S.; Business Conditions Digest.*
Federal Reserve System: business indices; charts on bank credit, money rates and business; quarterly survey of consumer buying intentions.
Department of Commerce: *Survey of Current Business.*
Internal Revenue Service: statistics on income.

Periodicals
Advertising Age, Chicago: annual market data
N.W. Ayer and Sons, New York: *Directory of Publications*
Industrial Marketing, Chicago: market data and directory
The Journal of Marketing, Chicago
Sales Management, New York: survey of buying power

Services
Standard and Poors, New York: corporation records; register of corporations, directors and executives
Moody's News Reports, N.Y.
Dun and Bradstreet, N.Y.: *Middle Market Directory; Million Dollar Directory*
Thomas' Register of American Manufacturers, N.Y.

Other
Council of Economic Advisers; *Washington, D.C.: Economic Indicators*
U.S. Chamber of Commerce, Washington, D.C.: *Foreign Commerce Handbook*
Some of these publications provide reasonably up-to-date statistical data.

The outlook

There is a computer in the future of marketing management. It will be used for:

Planning
Consumer and market research
Sales forecasts, economic projections
New product predictions
Return on investment in products and markets
Analyzing proposed acquisitions
Selecting advertising media

Control
Inventory information
Sales analyses by territory, customer, products
Gross profit; sales expense
Order processing
Routing of shipments
Advertising results
Marginal income; direct costing

Computer programming for such varied outputs offers challenge and opportunity—there is an expanding need in the expanding field of marketing.

Sales and marketing management will likely witness great innovative change in the years ahead, providing new jobs and demanding new skills.

Tomorrow's actions—NOW

As a marketing manager, initiate research as to consumer needs, buying power, demographic trends, and economic analyses. Master the statistics of market sampling.

Undertake critical studies into product servicing, quality, warranties, new uses for products and dynamic selling procedures.

Develop computer applications for many kinds of product and market research.

Keep abreast of new findings in consumer psychology and motivation; also of laws and proposed laws, that affect marketing.

Analyze and revise advertising, packaging, transportation, warehousing, and distribution channels.

Cooperate with your Research and Development department in devising new products or improving present products. Use both imagination and statistics in test-marketing them.

Set up statistical and graphic controls of all phases of marketing effort, measured against pre-determined standards.

At least once a year, question all marketing policies and practices.

Seek the optimum marketing mix (advertising, selling expense, and products) that will yield the maximum profit.

11

Who took the bookkeeper's high stool?

Evolution of the office

> When I was a young child I recall a photograph of a book-keeper friend of my grandfather at work in his office. There was a long, high table on which rested two huge ledgers. Over the table was a shaded lamp. My grandfather's friend sat on a high stool, wearing an eyeshade, which apparently was the trademark of bookkeepers of the day.

I SUPPOSE that the picture represented the status of the office in my grandfather's day. By that time typewriters and cum-bersome adding machines were in use. Several decades later, a number of office machines were available—bookkeeping machines, billing machines, desk calculators, and punched card equipment.

In 1963 I wrote one of the texts for the Alexander Hamilton Institute, under the intriguing title "The Office—Nerve Center of Management." Among other subjects it covered various kinds of duplicating equipment, addressing equipment, office calculating machines, tabulating systems and electronic computers. If that book were to be rewritten to-day, it would be vastly different in content, so rapid has been the change in office equipment and practice. The present is indeed a far cry from the bookkeeper's high stool of my grandfather's day. Today the office is recognized as a department for the production, processing and storage of information necessary for knowledgeable management.

The computer has become the strategic center of management. In some companies it remains merely a data processing activity; in progressive organizations it is the heart of a management information system. If it is merely data processing, it is probably accounting oriented, producing routine data such as labor, material and overhead costs; customer billing; preparation of accounts payable checks; and inventory control. However, when managers envision the computer's role in a management information system, it will do the routine things but additionally will take on unique problems, translated into mathematical terms; will extrapolate trends into the future; will undertake operations research or other complex computations; will evaluate alternative courses of management action; will supply top managers with data as to current operations or for making important decisions, and may have esoteric outputs such as maps, charts, and microfilm. Such an important tool of management deserves further consideration in this chapter. First, however, let us consider office practice on a more mundane level as it exists in most companies—even in those which are using computers.

In the early decades of this century "the office" was considered a costly but necessary nuisance—its labor non-productive. Despite this attitude, and because of growing demand for data and reports, the portion of office employees in total employment increased steadily.

Finally, it dawned on managers that the office was indeed a *production* department: supportive of procurement, production, and sales; accounting for money; providing cost and other data for managerial action; relating to govermental regulations; and gathering significant economic data.

As a production department, the office was susceptible to industrial engineering methods: time study, layout, flow of work, planning, scheduling, output standards, and mechanization. Office managers were largely concerned with selecting advanced equipment and devising efficient systems for getting out the work, and on time.

The computer was a bombshell. As always with innovation, some office managers feared it, resisted it, derided it—but finally accepted it as a "fast clerk." Rental of a computer even became a status symbol of progressiveness.

> In the mid-1960s I was conducting an employee attitude survey for a sizable life insurance company. One day the executive vice president, following a luncheon with his counterpart from a competing company, telephoned IBM to order a computer like his competitor had. No feasibility study, no systems analysis, no advance planning. The equipment, delivered five months later, was idle for another seven months, while the executive vice president served as the highest paid programmer in history!

White collar employees can no longer be taken for granted as loyal subjects in management's fiefdom. Union encroachment, discrimination against women, equal pay for equal work, and the boredom of routine tasks and low earning power compared with factory jobs have put office personnel problems on a parity with those in the plant.

Since many office jobs require higher education or intelligence than plant jobs, employment tests are particularly useful. However, such use causes two problems: (1) test validation—i.e., proving that test scores are "job related"—and (2) avoiding minority discrimination, since minority applicants may have less education or have otherwise been "culturally deprived." Training for office employees is mostly picked up on-the-job under the less than watchful eye of an experienced employee. Rarely does it result from careful job analysis followed by an organized job instruction program and trainer check up.

Most companies have developed adequate salary administration plans based on job evaluation and frequently including performance appraisal.

Office employees usually have repeated personal contact with immediate superiors and even with top level executives. This fact has undoubtedly contributed to the morale level, which almost always is higher than exists in the plant. Office jobs lend themselves to flexible reporting and quitting time, a fact which probably also contributes to improved morale.

Some office managers will merely become glorified bosses of office services; others will set their sights on computer operations, management information systems, controllerships, and vice presidents of finance.

Take your pick—but be willing to pay the price in extensive preparation and more-than-demanded effort.

The electronic computer

In 1948, IBM introduced its 604 Electronic Calculator, an outgrowth of punched card tabulation methods combined with electronic computing procedures previously developed at Harvard and the University of Pennsylvania. This innovation introduced the "first generation" of computers, which used vacuum tube circuity, drums and cores for magnetic storage, punched card input, and relatively slow output printers.

Improvements came tumbling fast from IBM, Sperry Rand, Burroughs, National Cash Register and other research-oriented companies.

> Let me cite a personal example. In 1955, and again in 1956, I took computer training from the four manufacturers named above. In 1968, I mentioned to an IBM salesman their 701 and 702 computer. "We don't have any such machines," he told me loftily, to which I replied, "You did once. Ask your research laboratory."

By 1960, a second generation had been born. Transistors replaced tubes, doing away with the necessity of air conditioning. Random access storage became available. Magnetic tape was used for fast input. Peripheral hardware was faster and much improved.

Five years later, the third generation became available. It included miniaturized circuitry, large disc storage capacity, almost instant retrieval, access from remote terminals and "time sharing" of large central processors.

Electronic data processing (EDP) includes the following principal elements:

1. Input equipment: special typewriter, special bookkeep-

ing machine, alphanumeric keypunch, tabulating card reader, paper or magnetic tape reader, optical character reader, etc.

2. Computer: console, processing unit, storage (memory)

3. Output equipment: same as input, plus printer, card or paper tape punch, electro-mechanical plotter, microfilmer, cathode ray tube for visual display.

The above three are frequently known as "hardware."

4. "Software": programs, translators, service routines, diagnostic routines.

5. Tabulating cards, paper tape, and magnetic tape can be used for input, or created as output and/or storage.

6. "Printed" continuous sheets or pre-printed forms.

Business is discovering hundreds of computer applications.

Prior to writing this book, I wrote to eleven acquaintances, each of whom was a recognized authority in his field, asking for a forecast. Unexpectedly, each one foresaw some kind of computer application in his specialization.

Current EDP applications include:

1. Routine clerical and accounting procedures, such as billing, payroll, check issuance, cost accounting, general accounting, inventory maintenance, sales analysis, various statistics.

2. Research, such as market data, critical path reporting, and extensive manipulation of available goverment data.

3. Decision-making by managers, including return on investment, distribution channels, sales forecasts, long range planning, simulation systems design, probability estimates, etc.

4. Storage of vast technical information with fast retrieval.

5. Scientific problem solving, such as calculations in mechanical or electrical design, space exploration, etc.

6. Medical diagnosis.

7. Forecasts of weather, demography, economics, political science, etc.

The future will see many other applications; and probably equipment possessing a kind of logical thinking, or even some creative ability.

Computer-created problems

Even as the computer solves some problems it is creating others:

1. In big government, in addition to the plethoric paperwork, the computer contributes to bureaucracy and impersonality.

2. By maintaining dossiers on millions of citizens, the computer can lend its facilities to the evolution of an autocratic, iron-fisted welfare state, far removed from the democracy envisioned by our founding fathers. Because this invasion of privacy is scattered among so many private and public sources, few persons realize its extent.

3. By fragmenting and dehumanizing paperwork tasks it is making many office jobs routine and boring, resulting in the same kind of apathy suffered by many assembly line workers in the plant.

4. Executives who accept computer results without question are often substituting the initiating programmer's narrow understanding of a problem for their own experience and judgment.

5. Computer errors, in billing for example, are frustrating and can unjustly impair an individual's credit standing.

6. It is becoming increasingly difficult for the human mind to understand and control the capacity and complexity of a huge computer which can store a trillion "bits" of information and do 200 million operations in a second!

7. In big corporations, it is spewing out tons of records which few managers find the time to analyze.

> Several years ago, in the office of a busy sales manager he pointed to a pile of computer printouts on his desk. "These," he said, "are sales analyses for the last three months. They contain valuable information about products, dealers, territories, and salesmen. But there is so much data that I can't take the time to go through it to dig out what is useful. What should I do with it?" I suggested two approaches: (1) have an assistant study the material and mark significant items with a red pencil; or (2) use the exception principle. To do this, the sales manager would establish upper (good) and lower (poor) limits of sales by products, dealers, territories, and salesmen.

The computer would be programmed to print only items above the upper, or below the lower, limits. However, detailed information would go to the salesmen, and accumulated information would be kept in the accounting department.

Computer developments are moving in two distinct and almost opposite directions: (1) mini-computers for limited use by managers at lower levels; and (2) giant computers that can share time with many companies or scientific users. For example, in Philadelphia there is a University City Science Center supported by 27 colleges, universities, medical schools, and others. These organizations and numerous science-oriented tenants have access to a large computer. Similar centers are being developed over the entire country, largely to bring worldwide knowledge to bear on technical and social problems.

Teleprocessing is the term applied to the transmission of data for computer processing by means of terminal equipment located at points of origin. IBM and Teletype Corporation manufacture about half the 600,000 terminals tied in with computers in the U.S. Soon, many cash registers and bank teller stations will have terminals; probably Touch-Tone telephones will be adaptable as teleprocessing terminals. It is a fast growing field.

Developments like those obviously offer great opportunity to qualified personnel. Such individuals need to be more than analyzers, programmers, and operators of electronic computers; in addition they must be able to grasp the scope of a problem, and to develop mathematical models. Hence one type of large opportunity in the future is for mathematicians who will learn all about computers.

During my first year in business, fresh from college, I became imbued with the many possibilities of applying mathematics to business. Alas, my superiors were content with averages, costs and ratios—all of which hid many fallacies. Gradually a new generation of managers accepted such concepts as break-even point, cost variances, ratio charts, medians, quality control analysis, sampling, mathematical forecasting, and operations research. With the advent of the computer more advanced applications of mathematics became possible, such as simulation, return on investment, game theory, critical path programming, and regression predictions.

If you want to apply statistics to management decisions, you should master the following, *at a minimum:*

1. Time series—index numbers, link relatives, secular trends, cyclical variations, seasonal fluctuations, graphic charts.

2. Single variables—distribution curve; average, median, mode; range, average deviation, standard deviation, standard error, probable error, probability; curves of first, second, and third degrees.

3. Two or more variables—correlations, regressions, graphic correlations and regressions.

In a given company, the ability to instruct department heads as to the capabilities of computers will be important. Included will be teaching department heads how to find computer applications for their respective functions.

The manager of electronic data processing must develop ways to protect the privacy of the information stored in the computer. He will also need to keep track of impending and existing legislation pertaining to the operation of computers. The computer manager must be a part of the management team and not merely an operator of computer equipment.

Management information systems

Traditional management has been synthetic, its logic inductive: the end result of company effort was an average of positive and negative inputs from financing, buying, production, selling, recording, managing, etc.

The management information system (MIS) concept is analytic, its logic deductive: a company is a complex system that consists of sub-systems. How well it functions depends on the articulation of properly functioning parts.

Traditional management has been accounting oriented; the new management is information oriented, a broader concept. Accountants deal with collected internal data; managers with internal and external data, *plus* attitudes, people behavior, trends, policies, laws, goals, and anticipated futures.

Obviously, data collection to calculate annual profits is a simpler procedure than to meet the broader needs of a management information system.

Combining office trends with management information systems predicated on use of the computer, I foresee adminstrative processing centers that will absorb office functions such as stenography, typing, filing, copying, telephone; will handle accounting including payroll, accounts receivable, accounts payable, inventory, etc.; will store and offer fast retrieval of internal and comprehensive external data; will identify malfunctioning of overgrown or underdeveloped sub-systems; will aid in decision making and long range planning. The managers of such highly sophisticated administrative processing centers may well become the top executives of the future. The chairman of one huge corporation has been quoted as saying, "The next Chairman of the Board will be a giant computer."

In the public sector, such managers will be high level civil servants, capable of supplying valuable information and counsel to legislative bodies, the courts and the executive branch. Conceivably they will lessen confusion and conflict among these three goverment sectors.

The social implications of highly complex computer centers are vast. They can make available great knowledge for the solution of economic and social problems. They could also make it possible for an elitist class of rulers to subjugate or at least to control the lives of millions of citizens. The electronic computer may prove to be a tool in the hands of a benign big brother, or in the tightening talons of a man-created bureaucratic Frankenstein.

A concept of the ultimate computer is fantastically awesome. Even now it has been taught to improve itself, to translate foreign languages, to create music, to concoct new brand names, to predict possible futures, and to decide among alternative courses of action. It may enable man to explore other worlds, locate new earth resources, create utterly new materials, provide a common language for international communication, solve famines, conquer disease, make wars obsolete, control world-wide automated production, plan balanced world-wide distribution, and augment our knowledge of puzzling psychic phenomena.

Phantasies? Maybe. "Dream no little dreams; they have no power to stir the imaginations of men."

Tomorrow's actions—NOW

Manage office employees by organizing, planning, directing, and controlling their activities.

Use validated employment tests in selecting office employees.

Outline a training program for each new office employee, fitted to his qualifications—and check that the program is followed.

Apply to your office productivity much the same techniques as in manufacturing.

Consider whether programmed desk calculators might be adequate for some tasks now performed by mini-computers or a central computer.

Keep up to date on computer developments which might save in rental or investment costs.

Consider computer time sharing and service bureaus vs. having your own computer installation.

Before computerizing office procedures, simplify and routinize them.

List the problems that might ensue with the introduction of computers in your company (or change to larger equipment than now used.) Include ways to avoid bureaucracy and too much paper work.

Study the fast growing applications of mathematics to varied management problems.

Point office changes toward a future "administrative processing center."

Study information needs in your company: kind, place, and time; also storage and retrieval.

part four

Tomorrow's environment

12

Inflation—what is tomorrow worth?

"The communal keg"

Some years ago I had working for me a young man whose parents had emigrated from central Europe. When his sister was about to be married, the parents decided to follow a custom of the old country, namely the communal keg. Under this custom, each wedding guest brought a bottle of wine which was poured into the keg. After the ceremony all guests were to participate in the communal wine. The young man told me that the guests did as expected but that when the ceremony was over, they drew clear water only from the keg—each guest had thought that in all that quantity of wine the fact that he only put in water would remain unnoticed.

HERE is a fundamental lesson in economics. If goods and services are not made available, they cannot be distributed to consumers. There is an implication here for inflation also; if each contributor tries to take from the general economy more than he puts in, inflation must result.

There are many factors that contribute to the inflationary spiral, wherein the dollar buys less and less of more and more. Principally they are government, business, and labor.

The part government plays is extremely complex. Funda-

159

mentally if the government spends more than it takes in, it must borrow and thereby increase the national debt, so passing the burden on to succeeding generations. Every so often Congress raises the limit of the national debt, a ceiling which in theory was supposed to prevent overspending by government.

The government can increase taxes, a move highly unpopular with voters and therefore with politicians. Hence, instead of increasing direct taxes, such as income or property taxes, most governmental units, whether federal, state, or local, prefer to put the onus of tax collection on business, which must thereafter add to the price of its products or services. American business employs 85 percent of people at work and pays about half its earnings as taxes which help support government employees.

The federal government, through the Federal Reserve Board can control both the amount of money in circulation and the rate of credit. Raising or lowering the discount rate has the effect of getting member banks to raise or lower prime and other lending rates. Raising the interest that must be paid on bank loans has the effect of reducing the demand for further loans and hence of slowing down inflation.

The federal government can issue what is euphemistically known as printing press money. Such printing is a temptation which few nations can resist, especially in time of war. During the Civil War, the United States issued huge quantities of money termed "greenbacks" to pay for war materiel. During and following World War I, many European nations, Germany in particular, issued inflationary fiat money.

The writings of a British economist John Maynard Keynes have influenced the political leaders of many nations. Originally a classical economist, he changed his views radically and in 1936 published *The General Theory of Employment, Interest and Money.* In it, he advanced the theory that a government can safely print inflationary money for deficit spending, by regulating the interest rate.

Opponents of this theory say that it debauches the U.S. currency, subtly erodes the wealth of private citizens, and will ultimately destroy our free enterprise system.

In periods of business recession, governments pump printing press money into the economy to pay for public works projects, large contracts, increasing unemployment benefits and other hopefully stimulating measures (once termed "priming the pump"). These governmental actions undoubtedly cushion the shock of economic depression, but they also provide monetary fuel for added inflation, by putting more money in consumer hands but with no more goods to spend it on.

Popular political demagoguery ascribes inflation to the machinations of the wealthy. "Soak the rich" is a vote-getting shibboleth of soapbox orators. They recite some awesome statistics: the top 10 percent of our population own 56 percent of the wealth and get 29 percent of the income, largely as salary, interest, dividends, and rents. In contrast, the bottom 10 percent are in debt as to wealth and receive about 1 percent of total income, principally in wages. Despite taxes and share-the-wealth plans of legislators, as the standard of living rises, the rich get richer faster.

Wealthy families, foundations, and trusts have their funds invested about as follows: common and preferred stock, 43 percent; real estate, 25 percent; cash, 9 percent; bonds, mortgages, and notes, 10 percent; and other investments, 13 percent.

The wealthy can spend much of their income but only a small portion of their wealth; the remainder of the wealth, invested, provides jobs, goods and services for millions of people. Likewise, the spent income of wealthy families provides jobs for many persons. The money is not hoarded but gets into circulation.

If half the job-creating, income-producing investments of wealthy persons were to be distributed among the entire population, it would largely be consumed, not saved. Total productivity would then drop, prices would rise, and inflation would get a big boost.

Income could be more widely distributed without an equivalent disruption. Such sharing is the aim of the graduated income tax, minimum wage rates, and federal encouragement of higher wage levels. To a certain extent, these programs have succeeded in reducing poverty and in increasing the apparent affluence of the great middle class.

I use the word "apparent" advisedly, for the portion of gross national product that goes to labor has been relatively stable for some decades. Also, inflation can quickly erode a seeming increase in income. The problem is not so much how to cut up the pie (total production) but how to make a larger pie.

The role of gold

In 1933 the United States abandoned the gold standard as a backing for paper money, and many moves since that time have continued this process. The hard fact is that at the present time the American dollar is backed by only four percent gold, and even this gold is "in hock" to foreign creditors. As long as people have faith in the goverment, paper money is used freely in commerce. But history shows that when people lose confidence in their government, as when prices rise at an extremely rapid rate, citizens tend to hoard food and to buy tangibles such as real estate, diamonds, jewelry, art objects or, in our country, common stocks of gold mining companies.

At one time the role of gold in international monetary exchange was a stable one. The value of various national currencies in relation to gold became the exchange rate for trade. In recent years this role has been upset as most nations have in one way or another gone off the gold standard and allowed their currencies to "float." Attempts have been made by monetary authorities to set up some kind of international currency unit (Special Drawing Rights, or SDRs) but with little success, because the nations that set up the idea didn't themselves have faith in it.

The peoples of the world are reaching for higher standards of living. New born nations, still wearing their economic swaddling clothes, want the material goodies enjoyed, but earned, by advanced countries.

The "maggot of discontent" can be a good thing, if it is

translated into productivity; it is good to itch for things, but better to scratch for them.

Some causes of worldwide rising expectations are advertising, the movies, television, magazines, and travel to foreign lands, as well as the natural struggle of most persons to better their lot in life and to offer opportunity to their children.

The plain fact is that as many nations strive to raise their own standards of living, they need more of the basic resources of the world, including gold. When there is not enough of these resources to meet all demands, prices rise; the wealthy nations get the resources and the poorer nations are unable to achieve their goals, so widening the gaps between the have and have-not nations.

Shortages of resources

A ready example of shortage is found in the world demand for food, as nations try to improve their diets. Set off against this hope is the fact that the world population increases about 75 million persons per year.

The United States imports more than 70 percent of its aluminum, rubber, cobalt, manganese, nickel, tin, and platinum—all needed for its manufacturing. And 100 percent of its coffee, which workers would agree is also needed in manufacturing! Worldwide there are shortages of the basic commodities, as well as newsprint, copper, zinc, magnesium, and various chemicals. Prices respond to shortages so contributing to demand-pull inflation. Industrialized nations are suffering from an "inflation psychosis."

In future years a new element may enter in. If climatologists are right about a global cooling trend, we may witness changes of weather which will bring drought to many parts of Africa, India, southern Asia, parts of China, and perhaps South America. The experts in these matters say that this cooling trend began around 1945 and by now has been confirmed with adequate data. They foresee not only droughts in certain regions of the world, but great winter blizzards in some areas and flooding on a large scale. Should these dire predictions come to pass, resulting in disease and starvation on a large scale, they will cause economic repercussions over the entire world. The ultimate effect of catastrophe and shortages would be increasing prices of many much needed materials.

The consequences of shortages on business and industrial managers may be great. They may have to find new sources of raw materials or new materials; their companies may be called upon for sacrifices that have not been felt throughout this century; peaceful international trade may be disturbed; despite all talks of peace among nations, the near future may be an era of international disquiet.

Companies, and particularly large companies, will be blamed for many of the world's woes. While there is yet time, managers should foster the spread of basic economic knowledge throughout our nation and indeed throughout the world.

In recent years, a popular political gambit has been to attack profits of oil companies as "excessive" while at the same time prodding them to expand costly exploration for more oil. Over a recent ten year period, earnings as a percent of net worth for all manufacturing companies have been 12.4 percent; for all oil companies, 11.8 percent. Even the "Big Five" averaged only 12.6 percent, with their foreign earnings higher than domestic.

Legislators must decide whether lowered profits of manufacturing companies, or higher productivity, are best for the country, for the latter is dependent upon profits (federal income taxes are, too!).

Two types of inflation

Economists tell us that somewhere between 60 and 70 percent of the cost of manufactured goods is paid out for labor somewhere along the line from raw materials to consumer. For services, as distinct from goods, the percentage is much higher. Hence a ten percent increase in payroll will soon be reflected in an increased price of either goods or services. Increased prices in turn cause new wage demands by unionized labor, which if granted, again add to labor costs and so contribute to the inflationary spiral. This type of inflation is known as cost-push inflation. It results from increases in costs of raw materials as well as of labor and other factors entering in to the value added by manufacturing. We had an example of cost-push inflation when the Arabs trebled the price of crude oil, which increase was soon reflected in the cost of gasoline and other end products.

A second type of contribution to inflation is known as demand-pull. Here the demand is greater than the supply and the net result is that prices go up. Beef prices, world wide, provide a good example.

So far we have talked largely about manufactured goods. However, costs of services are becoming an increasing portion of the average budget, as illustrated in the costs of medical treatment and hospitalization. Another services example would be the cost of entertainment. High salaries and profit sharing paid to entertainers, whether appearing on stage, screen, or television, are ultimately paid by consumers. Some forecasters believe that the post–industrial era that lies ahead will have as one of its characteristics, hedonistic self-indulgence. Such a future may offer opportunity for managers not only in the entertainment field but in many other areas of recreation.

Inflation is a worldwide phenomenon. Although it may be slowed up from time to time by recessions or by severe depressions, it seems likely to continue into the foreseeable future. Actually, it has been going on since the founding of our nation, at a growth rate of around three percent. The outlook is for an acceleration of this rate. In fact we and the European countries as well as Japan are already far exceeding a three percent rate. Future managers must take into account this fact of life in planning investments, in making contracts, in investing company funds, in considering the implications of legislation, and in heeding the clamor of consumers.

Oldtimers talk about prices in their childhood—5¢ for a loaf of bread, 8¢ for a quart of milk. Beef, 16¢ a pound. High button shoes, $3.00. A man's suit, with vest, $15.00. Passenger fare on a city trolley car, 5¢. Visit to a doctor, $2.00. Mail a letter for a 2¢ stamp. And they've all risen to their present levels in this century!

Despite these inflationary price tags, our whole standard of living has risen. People at the poverty level live better today than middle income folks at the turn of the century, and better than "high" income citizens of many undeveloped nations. Wealth and poverty are relative terms; the African bush native who transports goods in his ten year old truck is, in the eyes of his fellows, a wealthy entrepreneur.

Rising long-term trends

In a completely balanced economy, deflation would exactly offset inflation and would be measured by an undulating index of prices in a business cycle. In a perfect cycle, prices would rise for sixty percent of the time and fall forty percent of the duration of a cycle. In harsh reality, prices almost never fall to the level they had achieved at the beginning of a cycle. This fact results in an inward long-time (secular) trend which may be a straight line but seems in recent years to be an accelerating curve.

> In 1921 a large oil company posted a notice throughout the plant that wages would be reduced ten percent effective the first of the following month. The practice of wage reductions had been followed for many decades. For most companies 1921 was the last time when wage deflation could be accomplished by management fiat. The growing power of organized labor prevented wage cuts from being used in subsequent years. Instead, management laid off workers, so increasing unemployment. This practice meant that the brunt of a recession was borne by the unemployed, whereas those still holding jobs went virtually unscathed. We no longer have a way to let the air out of wage inflation.

Economists speak now of "tradeoffs" between rates of inflation and rates of unemployment. High inflation is normally accompanied by labor shortages; recessions by increasing unemployment. This relationship presents a dilemma to government planners: how much unemployment is acceptable to achieve how much reduction in the rate of inflation?

Inflation leads to an upward adjustment in the general wage level. If this upward adjustment were to be shared equally by all people at work, some degree of inflation could be tolerated without economic disequilibrium. However, upward adjustments in earnings are not shared equally—as has previously been pointed out, members of organized unions get a disproportionate share, other workers and people on fixed incomes get a less share or none.

One consequence has been that many union members and other skilled workers have moved up economically to become members of the great middle class. Many have moved to suburban areas, own their own homes, have two cars and are sending their children through college. These facts have made them more conservative, less inclined to strike or to follow radical leadership of any kind.

The money supply

Inflation, the result of many pressures and counterpressures, cannot be explained simplistically by cost-push and/or demand-pull. Money markets and international competition are two other powerful influences.

Money markets result largely from the interplay of lenders and borrowers. People and institutions with money to lend expect a reasonable rate of return but also want to be sure that their capital will not be eroded by inflation over a period of time. Hence in a period of fast-rising inflation they will be reluctant to buy bonds, provide mortgage money, leave large sums in savings banks, or make long term, fixed income commitments. Instead they will move their funds into natural resources or will buy common stock of companies that seem to have a chance of capital enhancement or higher dividends as a result of the inflationary processes at work.

Borrowers are risk takers. They hope to use loans for investments which will bring in higher returns than the interest they must pay on the loans. Or they foresee a gain in the value of capital that will be great enough to repay the loan and have some capital gain left over.

The government has considerable power over bank credit and the money supply. There seems little doubt that easy money and credit are inflationary. The monetarist school of economists say that "too much money is chasing too few goods" (demand—pull).

In times of labor shortages, businessmen invest more heavily in capital equipment, hoping thereby to offset the lack of workers. This practice increases the supply of goods and tends to reduce the demand-pull inflation of consumer goods. At the same time labor shortages are causing increases in labor rates resulting in cost-pull pressure toward inflation.

Capital investment carries a risk. Because of inflation, depreciation reserves set aside for replacement of equipment prove insufficient when replacement time arrives. Companies must dip into shrinking cash reserves, or borrow, to make up the difference. In 1962, manufacturing debt was about 25 percent of net worth; currently it is over 40 percent—an albatross around the managerial neck.

International interdependence

Inflation has been the rule rather than the exception not only in our own country but in all industrialized nations. There have been a few periods when the upward rise of prices was halted, the most notable of which in the United States was the depression of the early 1930s. Since then there have been a few recessions, officially defined as "two successive quarters when the gross national product fails to advance." The very phrase "fails to advance" implies an acceptance of some inflation as a way of life." There is no reason to believe that this way of economic life will change. Hence business managers must predicate their long range planning on the assumption that inflation will continue. Some may occasionally be astute enough to foresee a temporary cyclical downswing and plan accordingly.

International competition enters into the interplay of forces that make for inflation or an occasional deflation. There is increased interdependence financially among the nations of Europe, the United States, and in recent years Japan. This interdependence shows itself in investments from one country to another, in competitive trade, in the exchange of international currencies, including the fundamental role of gold.

High inflation in the United States can price products out of international markets. In addition, military spending abroad can cause an outflow of funds for which there is no tangible quid pro quo. As a consequence we may import more low priced goods than can be offset by our exports; combined with military expenditures abroad, we will suffer a balance of payments deficit. This deficit will be reduced or overcome as the same or greater inflationary forces affect foreign nations and/or as we reduce expenditures abroad for military entanglements.

A prolonged business depression can exorcise the demons of inflation but governments, particularly democracies, are reluctant to take drastic measures that result in austerity. Unemployment is a political no-no. Hence inflation seems almost certain to be a way of the future. Governments prefer to pursue expansionary, deficit policies, so adding to the national debt, which must be loaded on to future generations. Frequently, political leaders attempt to mitigate the effects of their own weaseling by instituting wage price guidelines, stabilization programs, and controls. The last named inevitably causes many inequities and requires an enforcement machinery of considerable complexity and cost. Throughout the histroy of all industrialized nations, government controls have been successful for short periods only and have ultimately failed their objectives—no government has succeeded in repealing the law of supply and demand. It can, however, control excessive power of business interests, organized labor or suppliers of capital so that there will be free competition in the marketplace as to goods, labor, and services.

As is the case with inflationary wage increases, our nation

has no vent to let the air out of inflationary government practices: overspending and printing press money.

Ecology and inflation

Other factors that enter into inflation are ecology—the tremendous costs of restoring air, water, and other elements of the environment to a better level; safety—the costs of implementing occupational health, safety, and related laws to industrial activities and to the population in general; social security—the costs of giving aid to an increasing older segment of the population; health insurance—the costs of providing health insurance on a national scale, which costs are yet to come; employee pensions—additional costs to be paid out by business for transferable service credits; and increasing costs for energy. Here a scientific breakthrough such as a feasible use of nuclear energy, or geothermal heat wrested from the bowels of the earth, or utilization of the sun's energy, may reduce energy cost as a contributor to inflation. Well publicised shortages invite glut or substitution.

Some critics of American business assert that companies are overstating profits with misleading accounting, principally price inflated inventories. According to these critics, profits should be downgraded for inflation.

Trade unions report their members' earnings in constant dollars, to show that what seem to be big wage increases aren't really big in purchasing power.

If corporations reported discounted profits, as has been suggested: (1) some companies would show low, or no profits, which unions could use to justify wage demands; and (2) Uncle Sam would have a lower tax base; to run the government and its welfare programs, the tax collector would have to take more of, or all, company profits.

On the other hand, there can be little doubt that inventory "profits" in inflationary periods yield a false sense of prosperity.

It is no longer sufficient that a manager master the dynamics of production or marketing. Tomorrow's executives must understand the socio-economic environment in which their companies operate. Only then can they safely chart a future course.

Tomorrow's actions—NOW

Do your part to disseminate economic understanding to your employees.

Study 10 or 20 years' changes in equity vs. debt financing of your company, and project their continuance for the next five years. If inflation continues, what are the implications of your study?

Consider the probable effects of increasing international competition to your products, and what steps should be taken *now*.

Since additional capital is scarce and costly, consider "ploughing back" a larger percentage of net earnings than in the past.

Dispose of assets, products or services that yield little or no financial return or cannot otherwise be justified.

For the last three years, estimate the portion of profits before tax attributable to inventory inflation.

Estimate the current replacement cost of your major capital investments, and calculate the accumulated depreciation for them. What management actions are indicated?

Determine how worldwide famine, raw material shortages, or other global catastrophe might affect your business?

Be alert to Federal Reserve Board changes in the discount rate; and to bank prime rates. High rates slow up the tempo of business, the stock market, public confidence, and inflation.

13

The not so silent partner

Rules of the game

OVER the history of our country, the government has taken an increasingly important role in the regulation and control of business activities. Principally this role has been in federal (to a lesser extent, state) legislation of three general types: (1) anti-trust, (2) labor relations, and (3) consumer.

Anti-trust legislation has been thought necessary by legislators to encourage competition and to prevent monopolies of various types. These attitudes are more pervasive in the United States than in other industrialized countries, in some of which cartels, which carve out exclusive world territories, are considered quite permissible. Much anti-trust legislation endeavors to combine law and economics, and often results in vagueness that must be interpreted by the courts. These interpretations have tended to update practices and to become more restrictive.

There have been three large merger movements in the United States, peaking in 1899, 1929, and 1969. Each of these merger movements has brought on a clamor for restrictive legislation, largely because of a fear of size rather than the existence of any proof that size in itself was harmful to the public weal.

172

The first merger movement around the turn of the century brought on the so-called "trust busting" by President Theodore Roosevelt and was strongly supported by farm groups, organized labor, and businesses outside the large merged companies. Two outstanding targets of the trust busting activity were the Standard Oil Trust and the American Tobacco Company.

The interval between 1899 and 1929 saw the financial panic of 1907; the inflation of World War I, 1914 to 1918; the depression of 1921; and the stock market euphoria leading up to the crash of 1929. In the euphoric period, important horizontal mergers were consummated.

The forty year period between 1929 and 1969 saw a long, deep recession, World War II, Korean War, and the Vietnam War. After the 1929–1935 depression, inflation was the order of the day. The latter part of this period saw futile attempts at wage and price controls on the part of the government.

The principal anti-trust laws have been as follows:

1890—The Sherman Act. It was aimed at business acts in restraint of trade and conspiracies among business executives.

1914—The Clayton Act. It was aimed principally at businesses where it could be shown that their actions had an adverse effect on competition in products or markets.

1914—Federal Trade Commission Act. It created a Federal Trade Commission designed to police unfair competition.

1936—Robinson-Patman Act. This was actually an amendment to the 1914 Clayton Act. Its primary objective was pricing practices. Since it tended to restrain mergers *within a given industry,* it had the effect of promoting conglomerates, which bought into many industries.

Fear of size

Although popular opinion is fearful of great size in corporations, neither the laws nor the courts have been able to demonstrate that size in itself is bad. Even where size was obviously being attacked, the government's legalistic posture was to prevent restraint of trade or encourage competition.

Some economists point out the beneficent effects of size. They say, for example, that large companies encourage innovation and so bring new and better products to the market place. They point to the lower cost per unit made possible because of volume production. They show that many staple commodities produced by big companies have not had price rises as great as other elements of the economy. They point out that some large companies even turn out products that compete among themselves, as is true with a company like General Motors. Likewise they believe size is necessary in order to meet foreign competition.

Despite these arguments in favor of size, the popular opinion is that size is inimical to the public welfare. Hence the institution of government proceedings or the mere threat of such proceedings restrains mergers that would otherwise come about. Other factors that slow up or prevent mergers are lack of available capital funds, a falling stock market, fear of impending recession, stricter accounting, and tax rules.

Despite governmental and economic restraints, mergers continue. If concentration is defined in terms of capital assets, then without question the hundred largest corporations in the country now have larger assets than they did 10 or 20 years ago. Much the same result is found if concentration is described in terms of total sales, financial resources, value of output, or number of persons employed. The trend to greater corporate size should continue.

Labor legislation

Labor legislation has largely been designed to regulate relations between employees and employers; to a lesser extent the operation of unions. Over a long period of years, laws have covered such areas as child labor, safety inspection of factories, restrictions on hours of female employees, minimum wages and maximum hours, industrial hazards, workmen's compensation, occupational disease, unemployment, veterans' rights, apprenticeship, training, and pensions. Recent labor legislation has covered such topics as conditions of employment, the right of employees to organize, unfair practices by both the employers and unions, elections, collective bargaining, mediation, arbitration, injunctions, the right to sue, and the conduct of union affairs. The principal labor laws have been:

1926—the Railway Labor Act. It guaranteed to railway employees the right to organize and to bargain collectively through representatives. It outlawed "yellow dog" contracts, whereby an employee agreed not to join a labor union as a condition of his employment. It set up a National Mediation Board and a National Railroad Adjustment Board to intervene in labor disputes. In 1936 this law was extended to cover airlines and their employees.

1932—the Federal Anti-Injunction Act (Norris-LaGuardia Act). It restrained courts as to the issuance of labor injunctions in disputes and eased the liability of union officials for acts committed or ratified by them.

1935—the National Labor Relations Act (Wagner-Connery Act). It set up the National Labor Relations Board for administration of the law. The right of employees to organize was reasserted and employers were obligated to bargain collectively with union representatives. It defined certain unfair labor practices by employers and permitted closed shop agreements. Its net effect was to increase the size, power, and financial strength of many unions.

1938—the Fair Labor Standards Act (also known as the Wage and Hour Law). It established a standard work week of 40 hours for most occupations and required payment of time-and-a-half for hours beyond 40. It also required employers to pay at least the minimum wage to be established by law.

1947—Labor Management Relations Act (Taft-Hartley Act). This law essentially rewrote the Wagner Act to restrain the actions of labor unions. It permitted employees to *refrain* from joining unions if they so wished, and specified unfair labor practices by unions. To implement the law it set up the Federal Mediation and Conciliation Service.

1959—the Labor Management Reporting and Disclosure Act. This resulted from senatorial investigations into improper practices in the labor and management fields. Much of it deals with the regulation of union affairs to protect union members. It is also known as the Landrum-Griffin Act (and sometimes as the Labor Reform Act). It placed further restrictions on secondary boycotts by unions, on jurisdictional strike activities and on union refusal to handle products of certain employers having labor disputes.

1963—the Equal Pay for Women Act, an amendment to the Fair Labor Standards Act. It provides for equal pay, for men as well as for women, where jobs are comparable as to skill, effort, responsibility, and working conditions.

1965—the Civil Rights Law. It forbids employers to refuse to hire an individual, to discharge him or otherwise to discriminate against him, because of race, religion, sex, or national origin.

In January 1973 the gigantic American Telephone and Telegraph Company agreed to pay $38 million dollars to correct past discrimination practices. Fifteen million dollars constituted a one time payment to 15,000 employees who, according to the Equal Employment Opportunities Commission, had suffered from discriminatory practices (which the company, however, denied). The remaining $23 million dollars went into wage adjustments to upgrade female jobs or to pay minority workers equal to white workers for the same jobs. The "consent order" opened the door for men to become telephone operators and women to become mechanics.

1970—the Occupational Safety and Health Act (OSHA). It required the Secretary of Labor to issue a set of safety and health standards for industry; the administration of law is vested in the Department of Labor primarily. It further provides for inspection of the employer's premises, for the maintenance of records, reporting of accidents, and penalties for failure to comply. OSHA is a far reaching piece of legislation, designed to place responsibility on employers for the health and safety of their employees.

Companies are discovering that OSHA standards can be beneficial. The Riegel Products Corporation of Milford, N.J., used the law as a springboard for a safety program that cut lost time injuries in half. The safety director says that the company considers OSHA as "a partner in safety."

Prodded by OSHA to greater effort than in years gone by, industry is spending about $4 billion for employee health and safety.

1974—the Pension Reform Act. It primarily affects workers now employed by companies that have private pension plans, insuring that promised pensions will be available at retirement age. It established minimum vesting requirements and sets up a Pension Benefit Guaranty Corporation in the Labor Department. The law does not require an employer to institute a plan, nor does it deal with the amount of benefits to be paid.

There are many other laws and regulations employers must obey. One of course deals with taxes and is enforced by the Internal Revenue Service. Another deals with government contracts and is spelled out in the Walsh-Healy Act. The 1969 Environmental Policy Act requires companies to file data with government agencies on the effects on the environment of proposed new capital investment projects.

The Consumer Products Safety Act of 1972 establishes a commission that can set standards, require label warnings, seize unsafe products, or seek criminal penalties for violations. Big Brother is indeed alive, and putting on considerable weight.

Various state laws provide enabling legislation for many of the federal statutes. Some state laws cover public utilities, picketing, wage assignments, union regulation, pension and welfare plan disclosures, and right to work provisions. Traditionally government employees have been prohibited from strikes and other work stoppages but more recent legislation has tended to ease these prohibitions and to give government employees representation, grievance procedures, and collective bargaining.

An overview retrospection of labor relations legislation suggests two conclusions:

1. For many decades managers have failed to foresee what society would consider their social responsibilities. Hence employers have been subjected to a maze of restrictive laws

to force them to do things, which, with greater foresight, they would already have been doing on their own initiative. As it is, when government has cracked the whip, executives have been forced to jump through a succession of legislative hoops.

2. Society, originally supportive of unions, has become tired of arrogance and reckless use of power. Hence it is moving in the direction of forcing unions to become a more responsible member.

Bigger government ahead

In 1949 George Orwell wrote a disturbing book entitled *1984,* which predicted that by that date, the federal government would be so all-powerful and all-seeing that all people and all companies would virtually be slaves to the State. In 1970 Alvin Toffler wrote a book entitled *Future Shock,* which predicted that the future of our nation in a post-industrial era would be so confused that millions of individuals would be unable to adjust to the changed circumstance. While I am not as pessimistic as Orwell nor as certain as Toffler, I am convinced that big government will get bigger and more powerful, further that social demands upon business will expand in many directions. We shall consider this subject more in the next chapter.

Typically, legislation is required to force business to accept responsibility for attainment of social goals. Typically, too, under our Constitutional system, it becomes necessary for the courts to decide as to the constitutionality of various pieces of legislation, or to interpret laws in light of public opinion. For example, soldiers, returning from the first World War demanded their jobs back and the courts as well as public opinion upheld them. This was the first time that employees were considered to have *job* rights, somewhat akin to property rights. The new decision showed itself not only in the rights of veterans to their old jobs, but also in seniority rights, a claim unions had made for many years.

Various commissions and other bodies created by law have in turn issued rulings and administrative interpretations, some of which seem to have exceeded the original intent of the laws. This was the case with the National Labor Relations Board, which swung far to the left until public opinion forced it closer to center in its thinking and rulings.

Many executive orders have the force and effect of law, without having had the benefit of congressional legislation. As another example of government intrusion on business: the executive branch of the federal government preempted radio and televison time, a practice initiated by President Franklin D. Roosevelt. While members of Congress so far have not been able to preempt television time, nevertheless they have little trouble in booking appearances so that they can express their views to large audiences. If business leaders want equal time, they probably must pay for it.

Controls of wages, prices, and profits have been attempted from time to time, with little success. In times of war or other emergency, rationing has been instituted, a practice that is accepted with little demur.

Developing is a fourth type of legislation affecting business which might be called social responsibility laws, typified by pollution regulations.

Within recent decades, public consciousness has become aware of the dangers of pollution to air, water, and land as well as improper waste disposal. Much of the blame is placed on industry, although municipal, state, and federal governments themselves frequently are offenders.

The outlook is that existing governmental pollution standards will be tightened, so providing a new kind of challenge to managers of the future.

Some astute business managers are taking advantage of the wealth of information and statistical data available in government publications. We have already mentioned in Chapter 10 the usefulness of some of this material in marketing research. You can get a booklet from the Government Printing Office, Washington, D.C., that describes hundreds of government publications.

Who among us can say with certainty that the actions of big government have been good or bad for society? History alone must give the verdict. What we do know is that these things exist and that it is necessary for managers at all levels to obey laws and to give heed to social trends as they emerge.

In recent years we have been assailed by a gaggle of prophecies from doomsayers, purporting to diagnose the pathology of a moribund American society. Some Cassandra-authors have nurtured a few germs of truth into a carcinomic disaster. I, for one, believe that the patient has a stout heart and a strong will to live. Turbulent change? Yes. Terminal cancer? No way!

Tomorrow's actions—NOW

Review your products and warranties against probable punitive laws to protect consumers.

Since ecology is in the public consciousness, study whether your company is guilty of air, water, land, or noise pollution.

Review company policies and practices for possible violations of recent laws on civil rights and discrimination; also on occupational safety and health.

Make certain that your personnel manager understands labor laws and keeps abreast of administrative interpretations.

Plan alternate growth patterns by vertical or horizontal acquisitions within your industry; by investments in other industries; or by increased sales and production of present products.

If you expect your company to grow by acquisitions, study provisions of various anti-trust laws and recent court decisions.

Learn to work face-to-face with representatives of various governmental bodies. Both you and they are part of a politico-socio-economic society.

Get from the Government Printing Office in Washington, D.C., a booklet that lists government publications; order those of use to your company.

14

Your business will be everyone's business

Business under attack

THERE is little doubt that business, particularly big business, is under attack from the public at large. People are questioning how business is organized, the way it has subdivided work, how it handles its employees, advertising, selling, servicing, accounting, and profits.

Supporters of the present system, including a few economists, believe that the corporation's task in society is to maximize its profits, that in so doing it makes its greatest contribution to society. They say further that any use of corporate funds for social purposes is in essence a tax on the owners, regardless of whether it has been imposed by law or done by executive decision.

On the contrary, a large percentage of people in general as well as leaders of thought believe that the corporation has a larger responsibility than mere profits. As a result of these divergent crosscurrents, management finds itself tugged in different directions, forced to balance the competing demands of employees, stockholders, customers, and society in general.

Some analysts believe that the corporation is on trial for

181

its very life. To a considerable extent tradition-oriented managers, concentrating on profits and exhibiting insensitivity to social demands, have brought about many of their own problems. If they continue to adopt the ostrich-in-the-sand attitude, they will soon lose their identities and become puppets of the state.

When banks on the east coast and the west coast of the United States change interest rates to the same degree and in the same point of time, people believe that collusion exists. Much the same can be said of prices of gasoline within a given area or of food stuffs and other manufactured articles. The newspapers hint darkly of inventions that have been put on ice by big corporations, of planned obsolescence in automobiles and other durable goods, or of worldwide machinations on the part of a handful of extremely wealthy financiers. The business page tells of over-capacity in one industry after another and the reader wonders at the investment judgment of executives which brought it about. Inflation—the result of greed, recklessness, unwise use of capital, government overspending, bureaucratic bungling, political manipulation, union power, rising expectations, depletion of resources and scores of other influences—is usually blamed on "profit hungry" corporations. Not one adult in a hundred has any idea how our economic system functions—but all hundred have the vote. Nor does he realize that our system is one of profit *and loss.*

Credibility gap

The credibility gap extends far beyond attitudes toward business. Some pessimists believe that the fabric of society itself is being torn to shreds. They cite the alienation of youth, disregard for moral values, enmity toward police, distrust of elected leaders, the apparent failures of education and religion. Black and other minorities see themselves as oppressed, and not without justification.

In this period of social flux, the task of a manager is increasingly complex. To survive, he must concern himself not only with making profits but with doing a lot of other things. These "other things" largely deal with the confusing relationships between his company and government and between his company and society in general. We shall here suggest four actions which managers can take to improve these relationships:

1. Consider adding a representative of the public at large as a company director. In some European countries this move is being forced upon companies by law. It represents an opportunity for a company to make a move in the direction of social change without waiting for government to force that change. General Motors has a highly competent black leader on its board.

2. Achieve greater employee involvement. This becomes particularly important in formulation of new policies or policy change. Employees largely feel disenfranchised as far as participation in company affairs is concerned. Some companies have put an elected employee representative on the board of directors. In Germany, there are "supervisory boards" consisting of representatives of shareholders and workers; company officers are excluded. Labor peace is said to be one important benefit.

Industry can never make all employees happy, any more than education can equalize intelligence, religion make everyone pious, or government make all voters of the same mind Industry can, however, remove many negatives: accident hazards, health risks, discrimination, harsh supervision, boring tasks, lack of opportunity, indifference to individual needs, insecurity, etc. In such a milieu, a small percentage of employees will grow, a large percentage will be content and a small percentage will still be unhappy.

Social accounting is a term being heard in meetings of management associations. It covers on an annual basis:

1. Personnel statistics—labor turnover, absenteeism, accidents, promotions, employee compensation, and results from employee attitude surveys;

2. Community activities—participation, contributions;

3. Loans of executives to government posts;

4. Legal problems, whether resolved or pending;

5. Social responsibilities accepted by the board of directors.

Some companies are including social accounting in the annual report to stockholders.

3. The board of directors, alert to the winds of change, should review all company policies, written or unwritten, toward employees, suppliers, customers and the public. Moreover, important future decisions should have as one consideration the effect on employees and on public opinion.

4. Reexamine all personnel practices. Our organization has made hundreds of employee attitude surveys that reveal clearly that although most employees like their jobs, they nevertheless are irritated by vague policies and annoying work practices. An unsigned questionnaire survey will usually bring to light scores of such minor vexations.

Management should encourage responsible dissent, a possible source of constructive change. Disraeli, the great British statesman once said, "All progress comes from the left." Merely to stay with entrenched tradition is to invite mounting opposition.

> The Saga Administrative Corporation of Menlo Park, California, based a large scale organization development program on the findings from an unsigned attitude survey of its middle managers. The program developed free communication between employees and their immediate bosses, and between those bosses and top managers. A new way of managing has been the result.

Involvement in social problems

Top managers should make their voices heard in community affairs, and social issues. If they remain inert, they invite self-serving politicians to place burdens upon them which ultimately place burdens on consumers, but blame on managers. It is too much to expect that at this stage of the credibility gap, business leaders can be considered as leaders of thought, for as someone has wisely said, "There is no leadership without the consent of those led." But if the statements of high level managers are in the public interest, those statements will be applauded by millions of people and so will tend to restore credibility. Business leaders should raise their voices in quick protest against irresponsible statements of left-wing rabble-rousers, impractical academicians, starry-eyed social reformers or self-serving political leaders. By consistently taking a "good-of-society" approach and by speaking out strongly in behalf of such a viewpoint, business leaders will ultimately reassert themselves as leaders of thought.

In recent years environmental pollution by industry has given business in general a very black eye in the public mind. Depletion of mineral reserves; strip mining; pollution of the air and water; and disregard of public health and safety, have all contributed to a widening credibility gap. Idealistic environmentalists sermonize on what needs to be done, but rarely discuss how, or whether people will accept the staggering costs involved. This observation does not mean that the costs should not be paid; it does mean citizens in general should realize that the costs of cleaning up the environment will add to inflation, that the causes of pollution have previously benefited them and prior generations, but that the time has come to pay the price of past profligacy.

Everybody wants clean water and clean air, but those who cry out the loudest for Utopia are likely to be those who have less to lose if plants are shut down, or if electricity which would have been created by atomic energy is denied, or if a past risk of polluting the ocean has resulted in a current shortage of oil. There are risks in all progress; in many cases there must be tradeoffs of benefits against detriments.

As an example of cleaning up the air, in 1952 in London more than 4,000 persons died from the smoggy atmosphere. This situation galvanized the city fathers to action. Today London is the most smog-free large city in Europe. The same pollution control program did an excellent job of cleaning up the river Thames. From this example we see that many of the problems can be successfully handled by community action. We do not need to live in the age of *e*ffluence.

186

Broadened corporate objectives

If future corporate objectives are to include a wider spectrum of social responsibilities, at least four criteria must be met:

1. Near- and long–term goals should be set for each additional area of social responsibility accepted.

2. Knowledgeable representatives of each area should be involved in both its planning and its implementation.

3. Funds and personnel should be allocated.

4. Controls and periodic feedback should be established to insure performance as planned and as scheduled, or to point out need for modifications.

Many boards of directors have added lawyers, economists, engineers, scientists, financiers, and management consultants to provide specialized expertise. In the future boards will include, or at least consult with, sociologists and ecologists and with representatives of labor, minorities, consumers, distributors, suppliers, education, quasi-public bodies, community leaders and governmental units. These ideas may sound radical, but are merely an extension of practices which have been in effect for many years.

Obviously new areas of corporate responsibility will open up opportunities for trained staff specialists, such as consumer service managers. Customer service units are often regarded as necessary nuisances rather than as ambassadors of good will.

> A personal example. The heating unit of our coffee percolator went bad. I sent a tracing of the unit to the manufacturer, a New York State glass works, requesting a replacement, to be sent collect or with bill. After four weeks, I wrote a second letter again with a sketch. After six weeks I received a form letter, directing me to order by catalogue number and to be sure to send check to cover the right amount—neither of which I could know. My reply sizzled!

Left-wing economists

Few managers realize that traditionally conservative economists harbor an organized liberal wing with some very radical ideas. They belong to a group known as the Union for Radical Political Economics, and they are represented on virtually every economics faculty in the big universities. They believe that most consumer goods can be distributed free; that profits should no longer be the incentive for production; that unemployment can be solved by cutting the work week in half so that jobs can be spread around. Additionally, all education and health care would be made free. To bring these about, these economists would take control of most of the nation's wealth and producing facilities by nationalizing the 1,000 largest U.S. corporations.

Radical economists of this school believe that capitalism has worked us into an impossible situation, with an inability to satisfy the essential needs of people for food, shelter, and jobs in a manner that accords with people's desire for peace and human dignity. They believe that government's economic policies are irrelevant to the things that are wrong and that those policies are merely leading us into class struggles and crises. Crime, they say, is a natural response to inequalities of income, in part resulting from industry's inability or unwillingness to hire or train the unemployed.

One of their tenets is that millions of people are spending their lives in dehumanizing occupations in exchange for goods and services that in no way add to their happiness or well being and in fact may ultimately destroy the environment. Of all the nations in the world, they feel that China is on the right track in putting the burden of self-sufficiency on each region, in reducing the gaps between city and country, between manual labor and intellectual work and in narrowing wage differentials between the highly skilled and the unskilled. They deny the value of rewards and punishments and see participation as the alternative. Although these radical economists haven't made much of a dent on our national life, nevertheless managers should be aware of their viewpoints, particularly since some of the current social trends point in the same directions.

It is not only the left-wing economists who express doubt about big business. A *Wall Street Journal* article (February 14, 1974) has this opening paragraph: "Every day, in every way, the large corporation looks more and more like a species of dinosaur on its lumbering way to extinction. The cultural and political environment becomes ever more hostile; natural adaptation becomes ever more difficult; possible modes of survival seem to be beyond its imaginative capacity." The author is Irving Kristol, a professor at New York University.

Management action sorely needed

You, as a manager should not wait for crises. The peaceful years should be the time for thoughtful change. Why need society cry out only when it is in pain? You must take heed of the fact that a given society at any one time reflects the needs, values, standards and beliefs of its people. It elevates to leadership those who promise fulfillment. You, in your own community, can see needs for social action. Through an employee attitude survey you can evaluate the beliefs and complaints of those who work for you. You can compare the standards you demand of your employees against those you apply to others, and consider what you should do if differences exist. You will be judged by the actions you take, not by the platitudes you pontificate.

For 40 or more years the idea has been growing in our country that central government can solve all social problems. This belief has been present in both Republican and Democratic administrations. Unless localized leadership arises on a grand scale, the future must inevitably see greater growth of central power.

Beyond local problems there are social problems on a national and international scale as yet unsolved. Many of them are easily identified: consumerism, ecology, poverty, housing, minorities, crime, health care, over-population, and corruption in high places. No one would say that it is the responsibility of business to solve all these problems, but few would deny that it is the responsibility of business to take an interest and to lend a helping hand, in solving many of them. Many thoughtful executives agree.

There are no simple answers to complex social problems. Federal aid to education was supposed to solve much of the ghetto problem. Welfare funds were supposed to be temporary expedients until people got "on their feet" again and went back to productive work. Help the poor by providing them with low-cost housing or free medical care; provide make-work jobs for all who are able to work; supplement the income of those who earn too little.

The mystique of such simplistic methods is no longer given credence. Large social problems must be attacked on many fronts at the same time. Housing, jobs, education, health, transportation, and communication are interdependent, mutually supportive activities. However, we must not be so idealistic as to believe that we can reach all people, or that all recipients are capable of rehabilitation or are worthy of being helped. Problems may be eased in a single generation but will likely not be solved in toto. Moreover, expectations are likely to rise faster than alleviations. Alexis de Tocqueville, a French historian, made an astute observation that is applicable. He said, "The evil which was suffered patiently as inevitable, seems unendurable as soon as the idea of escaping from it crosses men's minds. All the abuses then removed call attention to those that remain and they now appear more galling." In truth, social help for any given generation represents a balance between its expectations and its practical possibilities of their realization.

We have previously noted that our social institutions, including business, suffer from a serious lack of confidence on the part of the American people. In a 1973 Gallup poll, two of three persons believed that their senators and representatives won their elections by unethical or illegal methods. The same poll reported the following percentages of respect and confidence for eight American institutions: churches, 66 percent; schools, 58 percent; Supreme Court, 44 percent; Congress, 42 percent; newspapers, 39 percent; television, 37 percent; labor unions, 30 percent; big business, 26 percent.

Other opinion surveys have come up with about the same answers. People are unsure that profits, growth, production, and the gross national product index are as important as the quality of life, without anyone being quite sure as to what the quality of life means. Does it mean freedom, recreation, entertainment, religious devotion, possessions, status or self-fulfillment? The harsh truth is that these things will not be available to most people if business is bled by governmental restrictions, taxation, union demands, employee apathy, or labor shortages. These depressants will in turn limit the availability of capital (savings from somewhere) available for investment.

When a company makes a capital investment of 2.5 million dollars, the benefit waves are as follows:

1. It creates 100 new jobs.
2. It creates 65 other related jobs.
3. It supports four new retail establishments.
4. It causes retail sales of $330,000 per year.
5. It yields bank deposits of $230,000.
6. It broadens the tax base for maintenance of local, state, and federal government activities.

For some decades chambers of commerce and other organizations of business men have been urging their members to "tell the business story." A few have undertaken to do so but for the most part business men have been amazingly reluctant to be quoted, or to put the case of the free enterprise system before the court of public opinion. Such coyness has not been a trait of the detractors of the system.

In their schooling, most individuals have not been exposed to elementary economics. In the absence of positive beliefs as to the importance of business, many individuals swallow negative assertions of some self-serving politicians or the dreams of starry-eyed reformers. The greatest danger, however, spews from iconoclastic left-wing crusaders who would destroy, without having any practical substitute for, the capitalistic system.

During the 1974 diatribe against large oil companies, Texaco and others in full page newspaper ads presented charts showing profits, gross income, taxes, etc., pointing out, in Texaco's case, that only 35 percent of revenues were earned in the United States. These ads represented a good example of crying out only when hurt. Why should not the oil companies, and all other companies, be informing the American public all the time? It is a problem of candor and continuing information, not one of "public relations." It is a problem of plain talk and integrity, not one of accounting jargon and doubletalk. It is a problem of explaining the necessity for profits and how retained earnings, plowed back into a business, create new jobs and provide risk capital.

In summary, corporations, especially if big, suffer a credibility gap from the public-at-large, resulting from:

1. Fear of corporate power, tilting public opinion toward government control or nationalization. Note that nationalized industries in other countries are rarely (never?) as efficient as those operated for profit.

2. Suspicion of over-zealous, too-clever advertising and public relations gimmicks

3. Doubts of stockholders as to annual reports containing deceptive accounting or which overstates earnings, or gobble-de-gook to hide management boners

4. Actions of directors which glibly gloss over painful truths, or favor interests other than the legal owners: stockholders

5. A slowly dawning realization that managers are *employees,* and rarely entrepreneurs; that they should be paid for the high level jobs they hold, not for their ability to milk the company by nest-feathering bonuses, gratuitous stock options or fat retirement benefits.

The average citizen feels powerless to correct these conditions which, to him are iniquitous or at least inequitable. If management genuinely wishes to don the mantle of social responsibility it will take a long, hard look at some of its top level practices. Bear in mind that when the investment industry failed to police itself, the Securities and Exchange Commission was created by law.

Tomorrow's actions—NOW

Consciously improve relations with stockholders and investors in general—important sources of capital funds.

Point management actions toward *closing* the credibility gap toward business.

Audit your consumer relations practices, in part by studying complaints.

Support educational programs that disseminate economic understanding to students and to the public at large.

Seek ways to achieve greater involvement of employees and managers in work practices and in community affairs.

Scrutinize all your accounting assumptions and practices in light of current criticisms of the profession and the suggested revisions.

Consider adding to your board of directors representatives of employees and the public; study this trend in European countries.

Include a social responsibility program in your long range planning and allocate funds for it.

Involve the top executives of your company in community action programs and in opposition to those who would destroy the free enterprise system.

Prepare your own program of "social accounting" including a critical review of written or unwritten company policies toward employees, customers, suppliers, governments, and the public.

15

What will people need?

A look ahead

IN GREEK MYTHOLOGY, Pandora was entrusted with a box containing all the ills that could besiege mankind, but she was commanded never to open it. Her curiosity got the better of her and she finally did open it. I sometimes feel like Pandora when I am trying to peer through the keyhole of the present into the great void of the future. Unfortunately I do not have the prescience to see its outline clearly. Instead I shall attempt to pay attention to various significant trends, to study their directions and rate of change, and to hazard a guess as to the symbiotic relationship that will exist between these forces and business management. To my own views, and of greater importance, will be added the forecasts of sociologists and various "think tank" groups who operate on a more systematic basis than I.

The role of a forecaster is an unenviable one. If his forecasts fail to come about, he becomes the object of ridicule; if they happen critics, possessing 20/20 hindsight, class them as obvious! Moreover, prophetic warnings, widely heeded, become self-defeating.

We are here endeavoring to understand the milieu in

which management must function over the next decade or so. Since business management is probably the most dynamic force in our society, what it does and how it does it must necessarily influence the future; at the same time other social institutions will provide forces that augment or retard business, or set parameters within which business must operate.

The one word that would seem to characterize our fast emerging future is *disquiet*. If the world has no better business management or governmental actions than in the past, we must look forward to famines, tensions, riots, and civil wars in some parts of the world; monetary instability; and in our own country, mounting distrust of governments, industry, organized labor, education, and religion. While painting the dark side of this picture, I can add higher taxes, inflation, unemployment, energy shortages, basic material shortages, inadequate housing, urban deterioration, political indecision on economic and social problems, and continued environmental pollution. In such an economy, distraught millions could readily turn to a fascist-type dictatorship, should a strong leader emerge with wide-reaching demogogic promises.

I have purposely depicted a bleak scenario, for it could come about. Repeat: it could come about. The one thing that can possibly change it is *leadership*—leadership in government and business: dedicated, imaginative, aggressive, and upright men and women. Lacking such ideal leadership, we shall probably continue to endure worldwide turbulence.

A post-industrial society will strive to break the shackles of mass production–mass consumption technology. If it fails in this, business managers may prove incapable of coping with the complexities of the Frankenstein conglomerates they have created; government leaders may be paralyzed in trying to solve intricate social problems.

In this chapter we shall consider the probable future from the following angles:(1) family life, (2) religion, (3) education, (4) science, (5) government, (6) the domestic economy, and (7) need for leadership.

Family life

The home is no longer a dominant force as it was in our forefather's day. Working wives and moonlighting husbands, striving for higher living standards, have less time available for parental guidance; one by-product is greater tension in the home. Some parents become sacrificial martyrs for their children, causing loss of initiative on the part of the next generation. Some parents, looking back over their lives, warn their children, "Don't make the mistakes I did." In essence such parents have already resigned themselves to fate. If a high standard of living has been established by two working parents, and one becomes disabled or otherwise unable to work, the ensuing economic squeeze frequently causes frustration. In some homes, affluence is so great that parents and children go their individual ways, using the house as a domicile rather than as a home where family love abides. Credibility gaps are quickly adopted by children in their attitudes toward education, religion, government, and business. Managers feel the effects of these disruptive home influences on the work of their employees, without clearly realizing the causes.

There is an enormous pent up demand for better housing. However if the needed homes and apartments are built, they will require more electrical and other forms of energy than seem to be available for the immediate future. Moreover, mounting taxes and inflation will shove more families toward the poverty level, so widening the gap between the haves and the have-nots. Since population continues to shift from rural to urban areas, land in cities and suburbs is already at a premium. Rents will soar; since 1969, we have been predominantly a nation of renters. Minority groups, trapped in ghetto housing, may ultimately explode.

Our supply of food seems assured, but this is not the case for many people. All nations of the world are striving for an increasing share of petroleum, metals, minerals, and foodstuffs. Pressures are awesome in countries where fecundity outraces productivity.

Religion

For centuries, millions of people accepted their status in life or the hardships which beset them, as "the will of God." They endured adversity with fortitude: cold, famine, disease, plagues, and wars were the lot of mankind. But with rising affluence and increased education, many came to believe that there could be escape from afflictions attributed to the will of a stern God, a philosophy of many religions. Lenin, for example, called religion the "opiate of the masses."

In recent years trends in virtually all world religions have been toward more freedom of thought and action, with less didacticism or peremptory authority. Achievement of higher standards of living along with greater leisure have, in many advanced countries, resulted in lessened interest in church membership and attendance. It seems likely that this trend will continue and will invade countries which are semi-advanced industrially, as they achieve greater affluence. In the meantime sectarian differences among religionists have established hundreds of splinter groups, many of which should be classed as offbeat cults rather than as true religions. Should the future deprive large segments of the world population of *hope,* we may well witness a return to "the Lord's will" religion. Some hapless groups, having lost faith in mankind's eternal verities and virtues will dabble with witchcraft, black magic or other idiot-wizardry. In an era of ominous confusion, there will emerge soul-satisfying opportunities for dedicated leaders, clear-visioned high priests, who will anoint themselves with social purpose and be imbued with a sense of urgency to provide the new leadership.

Education

In each generation, education seems to be fitted to the vanishing past rather than geared to the onrushing future. This lag can be attributed to three major causes: (1) the past education received by present educational authorities; (2) reluctance to change on the part of all citizens; and (3) failure to plan for the future.

Few would deny that free education has been a powerful force in the development of our country. In recent decades we have witnessed more women attending higher schools of learning, and a larger percentage of our total population going to college and graduate school. Moreover, there has been substantial progress in the education of blacks and other minority groups.

In fact, college education and beyond became something of a fetish, a status symbol. Some employers have insisted on college degrees in filling jobs that don't require that much education. Unlike the views of our grandparents, manual work came to be considered as degrading. Domestic service in homes disappeared. Fortunately, mechanization tended to fill the void with materials handling equipment and household appliances.

Advancing technology brought on the need for technicians who could be trained in one or two years to operate technical equipment. Sometimes these trained technicians now earn as much as their college-trained contemporaries, somewhat dimming the luster of a college degree. The Russians have developed practical learn-and-work education to a higher degree than we. And Britain has Industrial Training Boards, which levy on company payrolls and give money grants to companies doing outstanding training in skills, supervision, or management development. Both unions and government cooperate in this effort.

In management, however, an increasing percentage of college trained people is found. This statement is becoming true even at the foreman level, where engineers or highly educated technologists are replacing the so-called practical foremen. As experience yields to knowledge, and since we are fast becoming a technologically oriented society, it seems logical to forecast that technically educated people will increasingly be in demand. In addition to such specialists, the highest echelons of management will require *generalists*—persons trained in many disciplines, as well as in the mundane functions of the business.

Scores of audio-visual training equipment are available, including programmed instruction and computers. More and more these devices are being made available for home education. Science centers are storing significant worldwide knowledge, making it available through rapid retrieval methods. The future will command almost instant knowledge in any field with the flick of a switch or by telephonic communication with a community computer. The outlook for education seems almost limitless. It could become one of the potent forces in shaping out future, if—or rather, IF, we have the necessary vision. That future is just over the horizon.

Science

In the late 1940s, technological change slipped into high gear. For example, it took 80 years to perfect the keydriven-desk calculator; 40 years to perfect the punch-card tabulating machine; only 20 years to perfect the far more complex computer.

Before starting to write this book I wrote to a number of acquaintances and authorities, asking them to forecast changes in their areas of competence. Practically all of those who responded saw an application of computers in their respective fields.

We shall see much greater computer power than currently exists, but with improvements in "soft wear" lagging behind. A large scale integration of micro-electronic circuitry will lower costs, improve reliability and vastly increase the number of users. The availability of EDP is giving rise to systems technology in many areas. For example, PERT and the Critical Path Method for controlling large scale projects are now pretty much dependent on computers.

In the mid-1960s we saw the beginnings of the present rapid social change. The cross currents of technology and sociology have given us today's tormented world of affluence and discontent. Both results may double in the next decade. Certainly the future will see an extension of man—electronic partnership in greater memory capacity; speedier recall; more accurate sensing; better computer weighing of alternatives; calculation of complex mathematical relationships too difficult for other calculating equipment; computer control of production facilities; faster communication, with large networks of worldwide information. Many of these features will be adopted by management; all will affect future management.

The field of mathematics has been given great impetus by the availability of the computer. By means of simulation, complex business and social problems can be solved or predicted as to outcome. The specialized mathematics of simulation has quietly developed to a point where society can greatly benefit from it. There is a National Gaming Council (c/o of National Bureau of Standards, Gaithersburg, Maryland 20760) and also a publication in the field (Simulation-Gaming News, Box 8899, Stanford University, California 94305).

In science there are scores of other intersting developments and break-throughs not necessarily related to computers. Laser technology, for example, has big potential in weaponry, communications and research; it also has applications in the computer field. Spinoffs from space research have resulted in 2,000 or more patents for practical devices that never existed before space exploration. Medical science has reaped a harvest from the findings of space research, which is also bringing us new knowledge about the oceans, the world's resources and climate. These spinoffs may solve many of our ecology problems before man's clumsy efforts achieve much progress in this direction.

Great advances are being made in synthetic foods, especially proteins. With a large investment we could capture solar or geothermal energy on a grand scale. The science fiction concept of robot slaves may well come to pass in "humanoid" types of production equipment.

Many of these predictions are coming from so-called think-tanks—groups of scientists from many disciplines who endeavor to probe the future as a searchlight fingers the darkened sky. These futurist groups, together with science centers previously mentioned, will pursue inquiries into unexplored areas of knowledge or will propose fantastic solutions which will cut the Gordian knot of once unsolvable problems.

In each generation, the emerging future must ever result from the struggle of chrysalis dreams to escape the fettering cocoon of reality.

Government

In Chapter 13 we commented on the growth of big government and its continuing encroachment on the business domain. The trend is worldwide. In many countries, government's power over business is much greater than in the United States. The term "friendly fascism" is being used to denote a possible emerging relationship between the U.S. government and business.

Although it can be expected that government will continue to exercise a heavy hand on business, at the same time government itself will be under heavy pressure to mend its fumbling ways. When government planning fails, people become disillusioned. When officials in high places misuse their power, people become distrustful. Hence one of the great needs of our time is strong statesmanlike leadership in government.

Many forces are tending to shrink our globe. Transportation and communication make for quick contact between governments, and between peoples of various nations. Multinational corporations transfer know-how from one country to another. Economic problems in one country are soon felt in others, frequently through the medium of monetary exchange. "If America sneezes, the rest of the world catches cold." Scientific findings soon cross national borders. Nationalism crumbles before international necessities.

The domestic economy

As was pointed out in Chapter 12, the outlook for our country is continued creeping inflation, but hopefully not galloping inflation. Inflation invites a scramble for power among various groups and sometimes rioting by sharply disadvantaged peoples. Our country can probably adsorb an inflation of 8 percent a year without dire consequences. However if the figure goes much beyond this, there will likely be severe dislocations and conflict.

In 1921 inflation in Germany was galloping. The government attempted to control prices of consumer goods. Mark-up percentages were limited by law, but the cost to retailers to replenish their stocks rose so rapidly that the only retailers who survived were those who ignored the law. Blue collar workers got raises insufficient to keep up with the cost of living; white collar workers and government employees lagged behind. So much additional paper money was needed that the government had to contract out the printing of such money. As soon as an employee got his wage-bundle of paper money, he rushed out to buy whatever goods or other tangibles were available before their prices would rise again. The process continued until it reached a point where 4.2 billion marks equaled one U.S. dollar! This horrendous example, still in the memory of oldsters, tells vividly what can happen in a runaway inflation economy.

Productivity is basic. It is the warp onto which the woof of man's intricate social pattern is woven. Managers of business, government, and other institutions are the designers and weavers. How well they function will determine the future social fabric.

The future horn of plenty will continue to pour out its bounty, but at the same time it may sound some sour notes. Economists forecast at least a 50 percent rise in productivity over the next decade. As always, this growth will not be steady but will be marked by cyclical swings. Part of the optimistic forecast is predicated on an anticipated increase in the working force of about 25 percent. This factor, added to increased capital investment, should bring about the predicted gain in output, despite some detracting influences, such as shorter working hours and more employees moving into service occupations or government jobs. The price-inflation, which will be tacked on to real gains in productivity, is something else again. Certain regions of the country and certain industries are expected to grow more rapidly than others. Slow growth is predicted for the west-north central and the east-south central regions; also for iron and steel, leather, tobacco, apparel, and metal mining.

Some possible sour notes mentioned before are the energy crisis, rapidly rising food prices, public mistrust of big government and big business, scarcities of natural resources, class conflicts in society, expectations rising faster than possible realizations, the demands of environmentalists that conflict with suppliers of energy, the impossible dream that all jobs be meaningful, and the decline of the work ethic.

Balancing out the positive and negative forces at work, it appears that our country will go ahead but at a slower pace than has been true in recent decades. There will be greater need for educated people, efficient workers, innovative minds and leadership in all institutions.

Need for leadership

Leadership in business and government, in its continuing search for tomorrow, must consider:

1. What have been the best aspects of the past and how can we preserve them for the future?

2. How can we not only adapt to future change, but plan for it?

3. What kind of future do we want to plan for?

In attempting to plan change, managers in both government and business, responding to pressures, come to realize that action is indicated. This realization initiates some such chain of events as the following:

1. An analysis of the pressures plus a study of existing policies, practices and organization structure.

2. A recognition of the problem areas, resulting in proposed changes or solutions.

3. A decision to attempt solutions on an experimental basis.

4. An evaluation of findings from the experiments, resulting in changes and improvements.

5. Acceptance and installation of the new practices or programs.

The remaining chapters of this book will be devoted to a consideration of the present managerial status; of advanced management practices already being tried; of large opportunities based on forecasts such as set forth in this book; and of the things a present manager, or a would-be manager, should *know* and *do* and *be* in order to qualify for those opportunities.

The important question is not whether you as a manager have the intelligence to meet the future but rather do you have the courage to attempt to shape it? For if you tremble at the future, you have none.

Tomorrow's actions—NOW

Study published opinion surveys to feel the pulse of public opinion.

Quietly determine how many of your employees hold "moonlighting" jobs; or are working wives or mothers.

Evaluate the housing available to your employees—adequacy and cost.

Critically examine your community's educational facilities and help in modernizing them for future needs.

Keep informed as to technological developments that might bear upon your industry.

Follow local economic indices, such as unemployment, bank clearings, and Federal Reserve Board data.

Subscribe to a research-based economic service, but check its predictions as events unfold.

Cooperate with government officials in their efforts to enforce laws pertaining to business.

Keep alert for worldwide evidence of disquietude that might alter the climate for your business.

See yourself, and all executives of your company, as community leaders—and act accordingly.

part five

Tomorrow's leader

16

Join the new breed

Management today

IN THIS CHAPTER we shall consider the present status of management, note some advanced practices, and suggest things to come. In essence we will be talking about what progressive managers are doing, or soon will be doing.

Many present day managers are both confused and disappointed as to internal information flow, data processing, organization development, management by objectives, and other modern practices. They sense social and legislative pressures upon them to develop the human resources in their employ, but have no clear idea as to how they are expected to go about it. Terms like job enrichment, flex time, and employee involvement are bandied about in management meetings as though everyone knows how to use these new management tools. Advocates of social accounting assert that it is possible to assign a dollar value to corporate activities intended to fulfill social responsibility.

In previous chapters we have covered many standard practices in organization and in personnel management. In this chapter we shall supplement these presentations with innovative methods that look to the future.

207

Organization

A manager should understand the seminal origins of present day management practices. I have in my library a 1962 book on management; in its day it was an excellent presentation. It covered the historical development, organization structure, policies, delegation, span of control, chain of command, line and staff relationships, policies, planning, directing, coordinating, and control. All these concepts exist in name at least today; however the connotations of many have altered considerably. For example, the new breed of managers is unconcerned about applying a principle such as the span of control; they feel that the dictates of each situation are paramount. Similarly, in planning they see it not so much as a method of turning out production in orderly fashion as a device for innovation. They agree with Peter Drucker when he says, "Planning is not a process to minimize risk, but to maximize opportunity at a tolerable risk."

Managers are experimenting with new organization structures such as those outlined in Chapter 3. These include high level executive councils, matrix organizations, production teams, or teams of specialists developed for individual projects. Attempts are being made to reduce the number of layers between top and bottom of an organization. Criticism is being encouraged, by first establishing a climate of confidence so that dissenters who stick out their necks will not risk losing their heads.

In the past some managers have instituted job descriptions because at management association meetings it was said to be the thing to do; once made, they were promptly forgotten. The new breed of managers is updating job descriptions and using them in a number of directions, such as establishment of standards for selection or promotion; content of training programs; the basis for job evaluation and performance rating; establishment of objectives under an MBO program; reduction of accident hazards and conformity to federal laws such as OSHA; publishing lines of promotion; job enrichment; methods' improvement. Such forward looking managers are viewing today's problems with an eye to the future, not looking at tomorrow with eyes of yesterday.

At a higher level, boards of directors are coming of age. A directorship was formerly a status symbol, and directors were expected pretty much to endorse the actions of management. With corporate growth, conglomerates, and international relationships, it becomes necessary to have specialists on the boards of directors and to listen to what they say in their respective areas of competence. Because of past laxity of many boards of directors, laws have placed more accountability upon the individual members, causing them to be more cautious in using the rubber stamp.

Modern managers are endeavoring to manage change. They are learning to indentify the growing pains (see Chapter 3) that suggest the need for change and to consider outside forces such as new technology, new attitudes toward work, and new social pressures. These forces are causing new philosophies of management, new implementing policies, new managerial procedures, and new methods of work.

The stiff necked "organization man" who did everything by rule and rote is fast disappearing. The new manager, and particularly the young manager, is interested in challenging work, in his own personal growth, in practices that permit the growth of those who work for him, and in open and free relationships with personnel of any level. As we pointed out in Chapter 7, the new breed of managers will endeavor to set up a better relationship with a new breed of union leader. Social pressures on both types of leader are increasing to bring about such a desirable goal.

Personnel

It is in human relations that the greatest changes are occurring in management practice. These changes are affecting selection, training, incentives (both financial and non-financial), and supervision. The selection practices detailed in Chapter 5 are being widely adopted, although the Supreme Court decision as to employment test validation has lessened the use of tests—unnecessarily so in my judgment. Test validation is not that difficult.

Legislation, back-pay awards and public opinion pressure employers to hire members of minority groups regardless of test findings, low schooling, or lack of experience. This situation has caused renewed accent on employee training.

The federal government has taken an interest in training. At first the U.S. Department of Labor was given the responsibility for training and had control over a few billion dollars of funds. Much of the money was spent on disadvantaged persons, many of whom had had no real educational or experiential backgrounds. In 1973 Congress passed the Comprehensive Employment and Training Act which provided several billion dollars a year in funds but turned over control of the whole operation to state and local agencies. In essence we see here another example where industry has failed to accept training responsibility and various governmental units have had to pick up the ball and run with it. It remains to be seen whether these governmental units can do an effective job.

Many managers fail to realize that excellent training not only produces better work on the part of an employee but it also tends to give him greater satisfaction in his job and hence to bind him closer to the organization.

During World War II the federal government called upon a number of outstanding personnel men to develop a nationwide training program. This program came to be known as the "Job Instruction Training (JIT)" program and it proved quite successful. Under it, experienced workers, serving as trainers, were taught four rules for breaking in a novice: (1) tell the learner, (2) show him, (3) have him perform it, and (4) check up that he is doing it properly.

This approach is excellent where training on the job is being followed; it deserves wider application.

Virtually all skills consist of combinations of knowledge, sensory observations, and muscular coordination. Audo-visual equipment, including programmed instruction, can impart much of the knowledge needed by any skill. It can also provide considerable sensory training, but it cannot of itself develop muscular coordination. To drive the motor car, to play tennis, learn to operate a typewriter or to become a lathe operator, the learner must practice with his own muscles. All that knowledge or sensory training can do is to shorten the learning period.

There is, however, a relatively unused method that will also shorten the learning period for muscular coordination. It is known as repetitive impact. Under it all operations necessary for the performance of a skill are first analyzed, and those that are particularly difficult or present certain "hazard points" are identified. Backing an automobile into a parking space would be considered a hazard point, as would serving the ball in tennis, learning the positions of keys on a typewriter without looking at them, or making a set-up for a lathe operation. The trainee practices the hazard points perhaps a hundred times more often than the rest of the skill. In this way he acquires as much facility with the hazard points as with the remainder of the operation. Hence when he puts them all together, he is able to pass the hazard points as easily as to do the less complex parts. The principle of repetitive impact has great applicability at all levels of business training and in all professions. Managers of the future will learn this principle more than has been true in the past and will see its application in many varieties of training work.

In recent years there has been a distinct trend toward training young people for new careers, some of which have resulted from new technology. This is in part a reversal of an attitude that one had to get a college education to get anywhere in life. Many individuals trained in specialized technology, skilled artisans, people in trades or service occupations have made out better financially and have been happier than some college graduates who have floundered after graduation.

Where individual training is being attempted, it is desirable to prepare a "training prescription." Under this plan, the trainee is studied as to what educational background he possesses, what specifically he knows about the subject to be taught, what practical experience he has had related to that subject, limitations of personality or physique and an analysis of his strong interests. Based on this background information, a program is outlined for him to fill in the gaps of knowledge, to give additional practice, to change attitudes, and to provide repeated motivations.

Group discussions are most effective when they encourage participation. The modern leader will not express his personal opinions but will elicit ideas and opinions from the members of the group, always, however, keeping their attention focused on the problem. Some leaders have members sit in a circle or semi-circle or around a long table so that there is no obvious leader or chairman's position. After the leader states the problem, he solicits ideas, even those that seem remote from the problem at hand. He will not attempt to dominate the group or to make personal comments on suggestions. He will prevent one member from interrupting the presentation of another. By careful questioning, he will get all members of the group to participate.

Incentives and compensation

Motivations in human relationships have greater power than compensation but we shall here touch upon both. In Chapter 6 we considered some of the findings of sociologists and psychologists. The new breed of managers is taking these findings seriously and is endeavoring to discover ways of applying them. For example, studies have been made of persuasiveness.

Most managers think they can be persuasive when the need arises, but they probably never analyzed the art of persuasion. Salesmen, advertising men, purchasing agents, labor negotiators, public relations specialists as well as foremen and managers will need greater persuasive powers in the future. Employees, customers and the average citizen have higher education, less respect for the "establishment," and less credulity than heretofore.

Authorities tell us that persuasiveness must take into account:

1. The needs and background of the "other fellow";
2. Cultural differences;
3. The art of listening to what he says and to what he means;
4. Interpreting facial expressions and gestures;
5. Communication—choice of words; use of questions; redefining issues; providing information;
6. Finding areas of agreement;

7. Avoidance of dogmatism; willingness to compromise;
8. Patience; low key discussion;
9. Involvement; joint effort;
10. Motivation—benefits to the persuadee.

Realize that the dominant manager is not the one who shouts the loudest—is rather the one who gets his way. Anyone who follows the above principles will automatically be creating good communication between himself and his subordinates.

> As an example of such communication, one of my clients, the Hickory Manufacturing Company of Hickory, North Carolina, makers of quality furniture, has developed a successful program of employee communication. Once each week, M. C. Turbyfill, vice president of manufacturing, brings together ten employees from various departments. At this session he informs them about new plans and progress of the company, invites questions, or raises questions himself. In the beginning of this program, employees were reluctant to open up, but after a few weeks they raised dozens of questions, which were, and are, discussed frankly. The meeting is followed by a one hour guided tour of the plant, which acquaints employees with what other departments are doing. The vice president says, "This program of free communication has accomplished to the fullest our desired goals."

As a different kind of communication device, General Mills has set up a "Fact Fone" program which gives employee-callers three minutes pre-recorded information on subjects of interest to them. It also permits employees to express opinions; to raise questions; or to enter complaints, which are recorded and which will be answered by later recordings on the "hot line."

> As an example of intangible incentives, consider the program developed by IBM Laboratory Communication Department in Boulder, Colorado. According to Kenneth A. Propp, laboratory administrator, the attempt is to stimulate creativity and accomplishment by offering recognitions, such as:
> 1. Photographs of those recognized are displayed at various locations around the plant, together with a statement of each one's accomplishment.

2. A short statement giving much the same information is published in the employee paper.

3. Those recognized, and their spouses, are invited to an annual banquet where they are honored for their contributions.

To qualify for such recognitions, an employee must have:

1. Been responsible for issuance of a patent on an invention.

2. Developed an invention to a point where it was found worthwhile to file for protection purposes.

3. Published an article or a technical paper in some professional journal.

4. Received an award for an important suggestion in some other program of the company.

The company has had the program in effect for six years and believes that it has stimulated employees, many of them technically trained, to achieve higher creativity and accomplishment.

The motivation provided by involvement is the keynote to a program developed by the Questor Corporation, a diversified consumer products company. It has established five criteria for its program, which it calls "performance management." Malcolm W. Warren, director of management development, tells me that the criteria are:

1. Employees must be told clearly what specifically is expected of them.

2. They must possess or be given the necessary knowledge and/or skill.

3. They are to be provided repeated feedback as to performance.

4. They must be allotted the necessary time, money and equipment for performance.

5. To use the company's language, employees must be "positively reinforced." By this they mean properly paid, recognized for accomplishment, allowed certain choices, offered opportunity to grow, and consulted in their respective areas of competence.

Much of the productive effort is done by work groups who solve many of their own problems such as goals, assignments to individuals, trouble shooting, vacations, safety and quality.

The role of supervisors is to coach and assist rather than to boss. All employees are paid on a salary basis. There are no time clocks. Involvement at all levels is encouraged.

We have previously mentioned that not all jobs lend themselves to job enlargement or enrichment and not all employees either want it or respond to it. Hence the new breed of managers is selective in attempting to apply job enrichment. They try to find which jobs and which individuals are logical candidates for such a program. This may mean a shifting of duties, in an endeavor to fit work to people.

Changes in working hours

Managers are experimenting with the four-day work week and with flexible hours (flex time) in an endeavor to find out whether they improve productivity or reduce absenteeism and lateness. Some companies have reported failure but most are making successful applications of either or both plans.

> For example the Hewlett-Packard Company headquartered in Palo Alto, California, has a number of plants where it has installed the flexible work schedule. Under their plan an employee can begin work any time between 6:30 and 8:30 in the morning and after completing an eight hour day can go home. The company believes that the program has been very successful and is extending it to other plants.

Managers in hundreds of other plants are endeavoring to work out their schedules based on the inherent nature of some jobs, the problems of line assembly, and other situations—mostly with considerable success.

We have here endeavored not to repeat some of the motivation practices brought out previously in Chapter 6. Rather we have tried to show that modern managers are making practical applications of sociological research findings.

As to financial incentives, most companies by now have adopted some plan of job evaluation. The two principal techniques are known as the point system and the factor comparison system; the former is simpler and more readily understood than the latter. However the factor comparison system is more flexible in that it can be extended upward or laterally to take in higher level jobs or jobs not necessarily included in direct production. Both techniques have been adequately described in management literature.

It is feasible to predicate earnings increases under either plan upon performance appraisal; the best kind results when judgment is made on elements of job performance rather than on personal traits of employees. The job descriptions used under job evaluation become valuable starting points for establishing management by objectives, described in the next chapter, which plan also utilizes performance appraisal.

Production teams are earning kudos, especially where they replace production line methods, as in automobile assembly. Usually such a team will include both older experienced workers and those who are younger and inexperienced. Versatility is gained and the generation gap bridged by the transmission of knowledge and skill that occurs.

Where production is organized by teams, the group bonus plan has considerable applicability. However since not all employees belong to teams, some companies consider the entire plant as one group, for incentive pay. Plans such as those developed by Rucker or Scanlon can frequently be modified to meet individual situations. Both plans have been well described in management literature.

Other companies believe that profit sharing is a better answer. Experience shows that profit sharing plans work well during periods of a rising economy but prove disappointing to employees in cyclical downswings. Experience shows also that the plan must be amended from time to time. Social and legislative pressures are tending to shorten waiting periods for new employees to become eligible to participate, to increase the percentage of profits allocated to employees, and to vest deferred profit sharing funds.

The manager as leader

Trends in recent management have tended to erode the authority of foremen and other lower level supervisors and to remove some of their responsibilities. Goals are frequently set for them by higher authority; working procedures may be established by engineering design or by industrial engineering standards; scheduling and routing may be determined by a computer-based production scheduling group; labor and material costs may be gathered through computer input terminals and not seen by supervisors until they receive printouts that show cost variances or departures from budget.

Recently the foreman has been told that his job is basically to teach and coach, rather than to boss. It is not only at the foreman level that new conditions are arising; every manager faces a dilemma: shall he be assertive and decisive or shall he be nonassertive and permissive? Is his leadership to be work-centered or employee-centered? Figure 7 shows that the range between these two extremes can offer various combinations.

Bearing upon his decision, will be:

1. *The manager himself:* what patterns of leadership has he followed in the past? Does he feel secure? Does he have confidence in his subordinates? What is his philosophy as to the role a manager should play?

2. *The subordinates:* what kind of leadership do employees expect? Do they crave dependence or independence? Do they have the education and experience to assume responsibility and decision making?

3. *The situation:* what demands are made on the manager? What is the organizational structure? How important is the problem? How much time is available?

The competent manager does not handle all situations alike, nor all his subordinates. He is sensitive to the abilities, attitudes, and independence needs of those who work for him. He gauges their group solidarity, or lack of it. Based on his size-up of problems and of decisions to be made, he will use one of the six orientations shown in Figure 7, or some modification of it.

Hence we can say that the successful manager is the one who correctly assesses himself, his people, and the situation and then applies the proper combination of assertive-permissive leadership.

The new manager is realizing that there is such a thing as

218

Figure 7
RANGE OF LEADERSHIP ORIENTATION

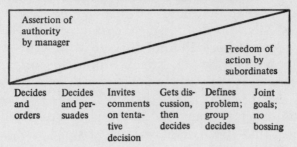

| Decides and orders | Decides and persuades | Invites comments on tentative decision | Gets discussion, then decides | Defines problem; group decides | Joint goals; no bossing |

human relations skill. Elsewhere in this book we have said that skill development results from (1) adding pertinent information, (2) sharpening sensory perceptions, and (3) repeating the required actions.

It is easy to understand how these three apply to training a machinist, for example. But they apply with equal force to the development of the human relations' skill needed by a manager:

1. He needs to ground himself in the findings of psychology, sociology, and economics. He should get background information on the people he supervises, works with (his peers), or works for (his superiors).

2. He should learn to observe and interpret voice inflections, gestures, evasions, tensions, "apple-polishing," avoidance, indecision, aggression, overt acts, health deficiencies, neurotic reactions, group pressures, etc., on the part of others.

3. Finally, the manager's actions can make or break his human relations skill. These include careful listening, judicial weighing of facts, tact in criticising, coaching, making prompt decisions, insistence on rules, support of subordinates and impartiality in administering discipline. By consistently repeating these and related actions, a manager demonstrates human relations skill and gains the wholesome respect of his fellows. He will not rest on his hunches, nor try to push himself forward by patting himself on the back.

Every parent learns that different children require different handling tactics. So, too, with a manager and his subordinates, peers, and superiors. If he will study the inter-personal needs of each one, he will be able to tailor his approach accordingly.

Managers are told that they must be willing to adjust to change. The new breed of manager is planning for and initiating desirable changes within his own sphere of influence before such changes become outerimposed. Where proposed changes seem to him undesirable, he should examine them with an open mind before expressing his opposition. Obviously he must adjust to changes which he cannot embrace, control, or avoid.

In one large company, I asked foremen and also higher level managers to rank in order of importance a dozen frequently found responsibilities. There was more agreement between the two groups than I had anticipated:

Responsibility	*Ranking by foremen*	*Ranking by top executives*
Goal setting	1	1
Methods improvement	2	4
Delegating work	3	3
Meeting deadlines	4	8
Planning	5	2
Checking work progress	6	7
Reducing costs	7	5
Discussing performance with employees	8	6
Employee health and safety	9	11
Handling complaints	10	10
Training (individual and group)	11	9
Enforcing rules	12	12

Note that in a forced choice ranking of this kind, ranks of 10, 11, and 12 do not mean that the foremen or executives considered these items *unimportant*.

Use of capital

If there is one outstanding factor that can make or break top management, it is its utilization of capital. Most of the important decisions faced by top management involve use of capital and frequently require long term forecasts. These statements—true in the past—will involve heavier consequences in the future. Interest rates, for example, are likely to remain high as long as capital is in short supply.

Worldwide the demand for new capital has far outrun the available supply. Housing, manufacturing, utilities, transportation, commercial activities, and various levels of government require vast sums for invested or working capital.

Companies get capital principally through four major sources: (1) Equity financing (*i.e.,* sale of common stock), (2) sale of bonds, (3) loans of various kinds and duration, and (4) plow-back of earnings.

Each method has its advantages and disadvantages, which managers should understand completely.

Because of inflation, reserves for depreciation typically prove insufficient to replace worn out (or obsolete) capital investment.

Capital results from savings. Hence, if company earnings suffice, plow-back is the best source, and is non-inflationary. Credit, on the other hand, can readily contribute to the inflationary spiral.

Many long range plans call for use of capital for intangible programs such as advertising, marketing, technological research, methods improvement, or social experiments. Rather few elements of management science help today's manager make such intangible investment decisions. We are somewhat better off in making *tangible* capital asset decisions, mentioned briefly in Chapter 8. Factors that should be taken into account may include:

1. The estimated return on the proposed investment vs. that from alternate uses of the money
2. Time to pay out (the usual rule-of-thumb criterion)
3. Pay back after the pay out period
4. Ultimate salvage value
5. Likelihood and rate of obsolescence
6. Possibilities in extending useful life of present assets
7. The mathematical thinking used in reaching a decision, including a standard of adequate return

The team approach to the study of proposed capital expenditures is desirable, so that varied specialized knowledge can be brought to bear on each decision. The fact that about one-third of the chief executives of companies in the United States came up through the financial route attests to the importance of the decisions as to capital expenditures.

The design and construction of factory buildings is being affected by technology and changes in management. Some of these new influences are tape controlled or computer controlled equipment, the location of computer terminals, the application of cybernetics to the feedback of information at various points in the production cycle, the use of production teams instead of assembly line methods, more stringent safety regulations, and attempts to improve physical working conditions.

One of the most difficult tasks faced by the new breed of manager is *technological* forecasting. In doing this he projects past trends into the future on the assumption that they will continue; additionally he gets the opinions of technical authorities, either in person or through published material, as to things likely to happen. Both these approaches can be carried to a considerable degree of refinement. Thus, the trend approach may be further analyzed into long time or secular trend, cyclical variations, seasonal fluctuations, and accidental influences. The use of authorities can be formalized by soliciting the varied views of individuals with varied expertise and getting the consensus of their predictions; this method is sometimes known as the Delphi technique. In the latter approach, the group may do extrapolatory forecasting by starting with the present or they may take some future end point in time and work back, to determine what must happen if the set goal is to be reached. Any company that has large expenditure for research and development needs to do considerable technological forecasting.

Trend forecasting alone proves insufficient, largely because of social and environmental influences, which may not have been present to the same extent in the past. Present day managers must look far ahead in forecasting demands for capital investment, especially in heavy manufacturing and utilities.

So far in this chapter we have considered certain large areas of future management, principally organizaton, personnel, and capital investment. In addition, major functions of the business have their own specialized problems that require foresight and decision.

In manufacturing, for example, these problems are likely to include production planning and scheduling, inventory, and cost reduction. The work of the industrial engineer is changing in accordance with these needs. Layout, flow of work, methods improvement, motion economy, time study standards, and similar activities of the industrial engineer continue in demand. However, his scope has enlarged to include operations research, mathematical simulation, and applications of the electronic computer to production methods. Computer terminal input is changing the way costs are gathered. Production teams are lessening the demand for standard practice instructions. Production standards are being applied to the work of a group rather than to an individual worker. The industrial engineer is having to become more personnel minded than was true 30 years ago.

Marketing too is feeling the winds of change. Advertising and sales promotion are discovering that they too suffer from a credibility gap. Some manufacturers are endeavoring to do away with middle men in the distribution process by selling directly to retail outlets or by using direct mail. Sales forecasting no longer is primarily dependent on past trends and market research; it must be correlated with technological forecasting, production capacity, likely availability of capital and a company philosophy that determines whether it will make what it can sell or will sell what it can make.

As managers become increasingly conscious of the demand that society is making upon them, public relations will increase in importance. Management is finding that it has a number of publics to deal with: consumers of its product, suppliers, wholesalers, community leaders, and, most important of all, various governmental bodies. The new breed of manager is increasingly aware of his public relations obligations toward these various pressure groups.

A distribution curve of present day managers would show

at one end those who are endeavoring to run the show as they did 20 or 30 years ago and perhaps as their fathers did before them. At the other end of the distribution would be advanced thinkers, who try to keep one step ahead of a fast-changing society. Between these two extremes is the bulk of managers, many of them perplexed by forces they scarcely understand. Principally they aim to please their stockholders by earning profits with an occasional inadequate gesture toward the community or society as a whole. It is mainly from this middle group that the sophisticated manager of the future must be recruited, in large numbers, and hopefully in time to save the free enterprise system.

Tomorrow's actions—NOW

Master the simple statistical procedures used to validate employment tests.

Join other employers and government representatives to set up community training projects to teach skills needed in your area. Supplement the effort with your own in-plant training.

Learn to lead, rather than to direct, employee training, discussion and "brainstorming" groups, and "value analysis" teams.

Update job descriptions for critical appraisal. Are they geared to the future, or only to the past? Use the information for many purposes.

Extend job evaluation to include office, technical, and supervisory employees.

Through study and practice, develop your powers of persuasion, especially in communicating with employees. Open various communication channels.

Develop foremen as guides and coaches, rather than as taskmasters.

Apply the exception principle to the work of managers at all levels.

Combine recognition of internal "growing pains" with outside influences to guide constructive organization change.

Work constructively with employee and/or union leaders for improvement of your company.

Consider the four-day work week, and flex time, for your company.

Make the company board of directors a working board, not merely a rubber stamp.

You, as a future-oriented manager, should understand capital: sources, uses, calculation of return on investment, the "present value" concept and discounted cash flow; also returns on assets and equity.

17

How to take charge

In recent years a new term has entered management's lexicon: organization development. It is a vague term that embraces various approaches to improve total organization relationships, largely by enhancing the abilities, skills, and attitudes of personnel at all levels. It is a long range effort, stemming from top management attitude and not a one-shot program, an updating of an earlier management audit concept.

The scope of OD is broad; it includes at least the following:

1. Improved communication.
2. Involvement at all levels, with a resulting climate of confidence.
3. Proper delegation.
4. Understanding of adequate planning relevant to each organization level.
5. Scope, and limitations, of decision-making at each level.
6. Understanding the pros and cons of various management styles.
7. Searches for talent at all organizational levels.
8. Superior training, including management development.
9. Management by objectives.
10. Utilization of management information systems.

Organization development endeavors to coordinate a great many human elements that can contribute to the organization as a whole. Many of these elements are mutually supportive. The whole OD concept can be likened to the human body, which coordinates senses, muscles, organs, circulatory system, digestive system, nervous system, bony structure, etc. These various parts, working in harmony, produce a sound body. Similarly the elements of an OD program, working in harmony, produce a strong organization.

The decision to undertake the OD way of managing a company should not be lightly made for it means permanent alterations in internal company relationships.

Prior fact gathering

The foundation for an OD program should be an analysis or audit of at least the ten points listed above. It should include a top-level evaluation of the strengths and weaknesses of all managers from the foreman level up.

An alternate fact-gathering approach is to use attitude surveys of employees and managers. This second approach gathers opinions rather than facts, but can be useful because people act in accordance with their beliefs and not necessarily in accordance with the facts of a given situation. As a result of the attitude survey approach, top management knows how employees feel about supervisors and others in middle management and also how those same supervisors and middle managers feel about the policies and practices of top management.

This was the approach followed by the Saga Administrative Corporation, mentioned in a previous chapter. William J. Crockett, vice president of human relations, says that "the continuing program has helped cure some of the alienation of employees and has helped managers with their operating tasks."

In previous chapters we have touched upon the importance of open communication and employee participation in decisions that affect them in their jobs. Some companies have stressed employee involvement but have given scant attention to the desirability of *middle management* involvement in goal setting, decisions, important changes, etc. Improvements in both communication and involvement are facilitated where there is a climate of confidence in existence; if not already in existence, fostering of communication and involvement tend to improve that climate.

Studies of the extent to which delegation has already occurred, or should be extended, need to take into account delegation of responsibility and authority, with the establishment of accountability in some form of control. In most companies the authority is lacking to make decisions close to the point where problems arise, so that employees, unsure of themselves, pass the buck upward. When authority is delegated downward, the right *and the obligation* to make decisions under that authority should be delegated and should be thoroughly explained to recipients.

Theory X and Theory Y, mentioned in Chapter 6 (and illustrated in Figure 7, Chapter 16), represent antipodal styles of managing. Extremes at either end of this distribution are rarely found; most managers insist on certain rigidity in production and at the same time allow certain freedom of action to subordinates. Organization development, through its many avenues, moves the manager's style in the direction of Theory Y; *i.e.,* toward greater freedom of action by subordinates.

Organization development is interested in finding additional talent internally, diamonds in the rough, at many levels. One simple approach to achieve this end is to institute a search for talent, discussed in an earlier chapter. It has been our experience that if 100 employees volunteer for the original examinations, the company will end up with five to ten individuals added to its talent file. We are convinced that there is a great deal more latent talent in organizations than most managers believe exists.

In this book I have previously stressed that most companies are extremely lax in their training programs. One result of an OD undertaking is to revive training at many levels. Individuals selected by a talent search are generally eager to undertake training offered by the company because they realize that they have been earmarked for promotion. Additionally, training in any form pays attention to employees and hence has an important side effect of improved morale. Employees will appreciate training to the extent that it is specific to performance of their jobs and this statement holds at the middle management level as well as at the employee level.

Management by objectives

Management by objectives can be undertaken without all the other features of organization development; in carrying it out, somewhat the same results will be achieved. We here include MBO as an important part of organization development.

Traditionally companies have been organized by activities and these activities are reflected in the organization chart. MBO puts the emphasis on *results,* and has variously been defined as:

1. The management of output instead of activity.[1]

2. A new approach—shifts the emphasis from cut and dried procedures to accomplishing results—makes overall goals the concern of every manager.[2]

3. Results-centered management.[3]

In his book, *The Practice of Management,* Peter Drucker suggested a new approach to appraising the performance of managers, which he called, "management by objectives and self-control."

Various advocates of MBO have applied the concept to

---

[1] Thomas B. Kleber, *Personnel Journal,* Aug. 1972, p. 571.

[2] Ernest Dale and L.C. Michelon, *Modern Management Methods,* World Publishing Co., N.Y., 1966, p. 55.

[3] Edward C. Schleh, *Management by Results,* McGraw Hill Book Co., N.Y., 1961.

different situations in industry, commerce, public service, education, and other organized efforts. In general, there have been certain basic tenets:

1. Job objectives should support higher level organization objectives, and should be reviewed or revised annually.
2. Managers, staff specialists and employees should participate in setting work objectives. Self-generated objectives and standards have more motivating power than those that are outer-imposed.
3. Objectives should be specific, attainable, and preferably measurable as to units, costs, ratios, percentages of increase or decrease, time, etc.
4. Responsibilities, authorities and activities should be aimed at the specific objectives.
5. Standards of performance, either qualitative or (preferably) quantitative, should be agreed upon by each job encumbent and his superiors.
6. There should be appraisal of performance, "feedback" and recognitions for successful achievement of objectives.

In applying MBO to team effort the goals are likely to result from team consensus. If the team members are given a relatively free hand in trying to achieve their self-imposed goals, they themselves will evaluate the competence of the participants, will designate natural leaders for various parts of the activity and will discipline laggards. When they encounter problems they will attempt to solve them by group thinking and may alter working methods accordingly. Foremen become coaches rather than drivers; in such a role, employees are likely to call upon them for advice or for decisions.

MBO is a new way of managing, not just a new tool. It brings about a hierarchy of goals; at the top of this pyramid are the company goals which may never before have been clearly understood by lower level managers and employees.

To make clear the distinction between activities and objectives, we list below 20 of each:

Activities	Objectives
Selects capable employees	10 percent increased production per man hour
Trains employees	
Conducts meetings	10 percent reduced labor cost per unit
Recommends wage or salary increases	
Plans work daily	5 percent waste reduction
Improves work procedures	20 percent reduced overtime
Submits reports on time	10 percent increase in dollar sales
Eliminates safety hazards	15 percent increase in sales calls per day
Insures condition of tools and equipment	
Inspects outgoing work	5 percent decrease in sales expense per sales dollar
Figures costs	Open two new territories
Handles purchases	10 percent reduction in labor turnover
Dictates letters	
Prepares budgets	20 percent reduction in complaints
Conducts market research	Double the number of formal training hours
Conducts sales contests	
Takes telephone orders	Double the number of job applicants
Solicits sales	
Prepares specifications	Double the number of employees given first aid training
Designs equipment	
	Appraise performance of all employees annually
	Get annual physical examinations for all supervisors
	Undertake annual long range planning
	Decentralize the organization
	Install an electronic computer
	Reduce taxes by 10 percent
	Reduce general and administrative expense by 10 percent

It will be seen that most of the objectives listed above are so specific that at the end of a given period of time it can be determined by measurement or appraisal whether the objectives were met. Other objectives must be found for public, quasi-public, and social organizations, as well as for various staff functions. Objectives for staff functions such as public relations, engineering, or research are likely to be qualitative, and evaluation of results likely to be judgmental rather than measurable. If a specific goal for a staff function can be expressed in specific words, a qualitative standard already exists. Hence recognitions and rewards for attainment become possible.

Implementing an MBO program

The discovered weaknesses of some MBO programs have been (1) the absence of enthusiastic and continuing support by top management, (2) failure to involve managers and staff specialists at all stages, (3) unattainable standards of performance, or absence of such standards, and (4) failure to correlate specific *activities* with specific *objectives*.

Figure 8 can help materially in overcoming the last weakness. This form can be prepared by the manager-encumbent; or jointly with his superior; or separately by manager and superior, followed by comparison and reconciliation of differences. Section C of the Man-Job Analysis calls for a self-appraisal by the manager-encumbent, leading to the actions indicated by Sections D and E. However, once the form has been prepared by mutual agreement of subordinate and superior, it can also be used by the superior for performance appraisal of the subordinate.

If decisions are to be delegated downward under either an OD or MBO program, those who are to make them should understand the distinction between a snap judgment and a considered decision. Hence some training in decision-making, such as the "decision tree" technique, becomes desirable. First the true problem must be defined; the surface manifestation of a problem may merely be the effect of some hidden cause. For example, the manufacturing department may be given a directive to reduce production costs, but further analysis might show that the sales department is pushing low profit items and giving large discounts.

Decision makers should be taught that once the problem has been clearly defined, other questions should be asked such as:

1. Who in our organization has the knowledge or experience to help solve this problem?

2. Are there outside sources that could be used for the same purpose, including libraries?

Figure 8
MAN-JOB ANALYSIS FOR MANAGEMENT BY OBJECTIVES

Name _____ Job _____ Date _____

A Insert five (or more) *specific* objectives of your job as column headings under JOB OBJECTIVES.

                      ACTIVITIES   JOB OBJECTIVES

B Below insert 10 (or more) specific activities of your job that
are fundamental to achieving the various job objectives.

  1

  2

  3

  4

  5

  6

  7

  8

  9

10

11

12

13

14

15

C Using a 1 to 5 rating system (5= Excellent, 1= Poor), appraise your own performance of each
activity as it may influence the achievement of all related objectives. Thus, a given activity might
be rated 5 in one objective column, but 1 in some other column.

D Study your low self-ratings to determine specific ways to improve them—what you should
KNOW, DO, BE.

E Write out your improvement program, with deadlines for various accomplishments.

3. Are we up against a traditional practice or a management policy that should be questioned?

4. What are the costs of the feasible solutions?

5. What are the effects of ignoring the problem?

6. What planning is involved in carrying out the decision?

7. What control or feedback can be used to insure that the decision was a good one?

Intuition and snap judgment too often are substituted for decisions based on comprehensive fact gathering.

> Some years ago, the chairman of the board of a large oil company was being driven in his Cadillac up a steep mountain road, when a small car scooted past them. The Chariman asked his chauffeur, "What kind of car was that?"
>
> The chauffeur replied, "Chevrolet."
>
> Upon returning to his office, the Chairman ordered that anyone driving a company car would, in the future, be supplied with a Chevrolet (excluding himself, presumably!).

Almost as bad as hunch decision making is deciding on the basis of insufficient information. In the instance above, the comptroller suggested a study of Fords versus Chevrolets as to investment, depreciation, trade-in value and operating costs per mile, but the chairman ruled it would be too costly and a waste of time.

Making a sound decision at any level is in part contingent upon adequate information available to the manager who is required to make the decision. To ascertain whether this information is both adequate and available, the opinions of individuals at the respective levels should be solicited. Those who state that they do not have proper information for job performance, should be questioned as to what additional data they feel they need, and why they need it.

The ordinary operating budget provides an excellent example. A manager should not merely be informed that he has gone over his budget in labor costs, but should be supplied the necessary supporting data to determine whether the overage occurred because of a great amount of overtime, adding more employees, or failure of employees to produce the expected volume.

Information flow, like the nervous system of the human body should pick up the input developed at each work center and should provide the output (*i.e.,* the information) necessary for proper performance of that center. As previously pointed out, the analogy is like the sensory and motor nerves of the human body.

However, too much information can swamp an executive who has never learned how to use the exception principle. This principle requires that only exceptional positive, or negative, data be brought to the attention of the manager responsible.

For example, monthly a computer produces 90 sheets of sales analysis data by territory, salesman, customer, and product, also cumulative to date, and compared with the same period, last year.

The busy sales manager cannot digest all this data. Here are two ways he can utilize the exception principle:

1. He establishes high and low standards for monthly sales by territory, salesman, customer, and product. An assistant reviews the data, marks with a blue pencil an outstanding figure; with a red pencil, a figure below the standard. The sales manager looks at and takes action on only these exceptions.

2. The standards can be stored in the computer, so that it will only print out data below, or above, the stored standards.

Management by exception conserves executive time, results in prompter actions—and fewer ulcers. Since it can be learned, it can be taught.

Executive development programs have been attempted for several decades. Many have failed, perhaps because of inadequate concepts at the beginning, or of insufficient follow through. Actually the OD concept is an enalrgement of the executive development idea, largely brought about by realization that merely developing better informed, more motivated executives with better attitudes was only a part of the problem; the remainder of the organization had to be lifted by its bootstraps to get the greatest benefit from the improved executives.

The president of one of our client companies asked his five top associates to rate a list of 100 items as to responsibility and authority. The rating system was F = full responsibility or authority P = partial, N = none.

The rating sheets were turned in to the president, who had them summarized. There proved to be many conflicting opinions as to responsibility and/or authority. There were even a few items for which *no one* considered himself responsible. The clarifying discussions that followed stretched over many meetings.

Although this effort was not called organization development, it was actually a sensible OD device.

There may be situations in which it is better to alter the organization demands on the manager rather than struggle to develop him in all facets to fit the job as it now exists.

One of my friends is a dynamic and imaginative production manager who will probably never become a good administrator. His desk is piled with reports, correspondence and a great miscellany, through which he has to paw in order to find anything. Each morning his secretary arranges his papers in what she feels to be a logical set of piles but inside of an hour he has them completely in disarray. However his company has wisely provided him with a methodical assistant who worries about procurement, labor costs, and voluminous paper work, while his boss circulates around the plant. The company has given up trying to make a good administrator of this manager; nevertheless production figures mount year after year.

Currently there seems to be reduced accent on manager development (that is adapting the individual to the demands of the organization) and an increasing accent on *organization* development such as described in this chapter.

Performance appraisal

Considerable research by social scientists suggests that judgments of generalized personal traits (quality of work, productivity, initiative, attitude, potentiality, etc.) are highly unreliable. The judgments of *specific* activities by knowledgeable superiors are more likely to be accurate; appraisals of *results* even more so. Herein is the kernel of MBO success.

The appraisal interview is intended to motivate those being rated to better performance. Generalized exhortations such as "do better" or "improve the quality of your work" are more likely to discourage than to motivate. But pointing out specific weaknesses, coupled with standards to be met and concrete advice on what he should know, do or be, can establish good communication between him and his rater, and lead to manager development. The hierarchy of such rapport at successive levels insures the success of management by objectives.

MBO can of course be applied not only to production management but to all other functions, including staff functions. Many top executives claim that they have been managing by objectives all along but studies of their practices show that the objectives have been so vague, comprehensive, or remote as to lack specificity and motivating power. The intent of managing by objectives is to make the objectives so specific and so attainable that their summation equals or exceeds total company objectives.

Obviously OD and MBO programs must be generated from and sustained by the very top of an organization. However they will need expert practitioners who are conversant with the techniques and will have the necessary persistence to carry out such programs on a large scale in a company. Herein lies another type of career opportunity.

Tomorrow's actions—NOW

Make development of people an important part of your leadership, using challenge; get ordinary people to do extraordinary things.

Conduct manager indoctrination sessions to institute and to maintain management by objectives.

Seek—and develop—managers with an entrepreneurial, risk-taking, innovative approach to their jobs.

Prepare an individualized development program for each key person, especially to fill out gaps in knowledge, experience, or personal attributes.

Take steps to correct excessive alcoholism among executives and middle managers.

Check the scope of organization development in your company against the ten descriptive factors listed in this chapter.

Ask managers at all levels to write out their responsibilities and authorities, marking each one F (full) or P (partial). Then compare the results.

Beneath each managerial title on an organization chart, write the job objectives as understood by the encumbents.

Make your manager appraisal system evaluate results, rather than personal traits, measured against jointly agreed upon performance standards.

Strive to coordinate personnel effort rather than merely to direct it.

Include "knowledge workers" in budgeting and decision making at their respective levels.

Personally visit companies that have installed management by objectives and learn from their experience.

18

The future belongs to
those who think about it

Know, do—and BE!

THROUGHOUT this book we have largely talked about the
things a manager should know and do. In this chapter we
shall talk about *you* and what you should *be* to qualify for a
high level managerial post. Social and technological change
has possibly raced ahead of your education, business information, experience, point of view, and personal development. In light of the many facets of the future predicted in
this book, you need to close the gap, or risk being unable to
adjust to that future. Survival of the fittest does not mean the
strongest—it means rather the adaptingest. The Chinese
have a proverb which says, "Great souls have wills—feeble
ones only wishes." In carrying out the suggestions in this
chapter you have a chance to determine whether you have
more wishbone than backbone.

Influencing your life are your needs, values, and beliefs.
To raise these to higher levels you require (1) strong dissatisfaction with your achievements to date, (2) the energy to
change yourself as detailed below, and (3) both short and
long range goals.

Many people have dissatisfaction and goals, but not the

will power to change themselves. Successful managers have all three.

The four factors of success

I know of no magic formula, no secret elixir for "instant success." The road is hard and long. Figure 9 presents a diagramatic analysis of the four factors of success. In preparing this chart, I have defined success in the current manner —earning power, advancement, prestige, and the joy of winning. We shall analyze the four success factors in greater detail below.

Figure 9
THE FOUR FACTORS OF SUCCESS

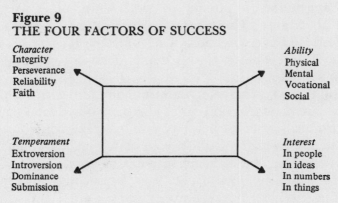

Character
Integrity
Perseverance
Reliability
Faith

Ability
Physical
Mental
Vocational
Social

Temperament
Extroversion
Introversion
Dominance
Submission

Interest
In people
In ideas
In numbers
In things

An increasing percentage of managers, professionals, and technical employees are stepping to the music of a different drummer than King Midas. For example, the American Management Association surveyed almost 2,300 American businessmen before preparing a survey report entitled "The Changing Success Ethic." The survey revealed doubt and disillusionment among many businessmen. For some their goals were changing from financial success and status to satisfaction from challenge, creativity, contribution to social welfare, and other intangible returns. These findings accord with the changing work ethic mentioned in previous chapters. However, it is my observation that these new influences tinge the success of executives but are not a substitute for it. Nevertheless, even if social aims some day do become the one and only goal of business managers (which I seriously doubt), the four factors of success here discussed will still be applicable. Character, temperament, abilities and interests are the foundations of a successful life in any sphere of endeavor.

Character

Character is an elusive term, but we have here subdivided it into integrity, perseverance, reliability, and faith. If you have integrity, you are intellectually honest, as well as honest with other people's property. Your word is as good as your bond. Persistence in pursuit of worthwhile objectives is a trait we all admire. There is no ceiling on persistence; once you have developed the habit, it becomes easier and easier to stay with it—the humorist says that a diamond is a chunk of coal that stuck to its job!

Reliability has some elements in common with integrity; you meet appointments on time, you pay your debts, you live up to promises. Faith can of course refer to religious faith but it can also refer to faith in your fellow man, in the rightness of things, in the ultimate triumph of good over evil and most of all, in your own future. It is the selvage of faith that keeps your life from unraveling.

Weaknesses in character traits reveal themselves as deceit, lieing, alcoholism, avoidance of responsibility, inability to concentrate, flitting from task to task, extreme cynicism, taking unfair advantage of others, cruelty, and unwillingness to help others who are less fortunate.

Developing your own character can never be outer-imposed. It is strictly a do-it-yourself task. An honest self-analysis will indicate to you traits in which you are deficient. Only you can resolve to improve them, and follow through to see that you do so.

It is normal for you to be concerned about your job and about your future. If you're not concerned about your future, you have none. Studies have shown that as people rise on the management ladder their anxiety increases because, if they fail or lose their jobs, they have so much more to lose in earnings and social status. As we saw in an earlier chapter, the Maslow hierarchy of needs suggests that once a manager gets beyond needs for physical comforts, safety, and security, he reaches for higher levels like social approval, self-esteem, and self-fulfillment.

In corporate life and in a rapidly changing world, job insecurity can rarely be allayed merely by high earnings. Knowing this, many managers have the strength of character to maintain savings accounts and make investments that provide both income and security. Likewise a strong life insurance program gives assurance that one has taken care of his loved ones. Some managers live up to their income with little heed for the future; character (sacrifice) is needed for the accumulation of capital.

Temperament

Temperament refers to prevailing emotional states. Moods are transient, but temperament is relatively permanent, unless strong effort is made to change it. Various researchers have developed different classifications of temperament but I shall here use the following:

Extroversion—Introversion

and

Dominance—Submissiveness

The extrovert makes new friends easily, laughs aloud readily, doesn't worry about losing, talks in a loud voice, is careless about personal effects, is generous, would rather say it than write it. His speech is fluent, he forgives readily, is tactful, joins various groups, likes physically active work, takes part in sports, seeks out the opposite sex, accepts supervision easily, doesn't hesitate to ask for advice, accepts criticism, likes to help others, doesn't worry much, is usually light hearted, is impulsive, likes exciting amusements, doesn't stick at one thing very long, starts new plans with enthusiasm but may drop them just as quickly, is sympathetic to others and believes that most people are cooperative.

The introvert on the other hand prides himself on being

candid with others, likes to be alone, enjoys mathematics, is a hard loser, likes routine work, would rather follow than lead, is likely to be sarcastic or suspicious, prefers to put it in writing, is close mouthed, may be stingy in money matters, is fussy about his personal effects, makes new friends slowly, seldom laughs aloud, hates to talk on his feet, holds grudges, likes reading and quiet amusements, is critical, deliberate in making decisions, argumentative, unsympathetic, takes great pains to explain his actions to others, worries a lot, his feelings are easily hurt, frequently rebels against supervision, craves praise, is likely to be a radical in politics, daydreams a lot, is extremely conscientious and fights his problems alone.

Of course no individual exhibits all traits of either extreme. In fact at least 50 percent of us should be classed as ambiverts, sometimes revealing introvert, sometimes extrovert traits.

At birth all individuals are complete introverts. Gradually they become aware of the needs of those around them and exhibit some willingness to cater to the needs of others. Schooling is an extroverting experience, as is marriage and rearing children. Throughout the first two or three decades of their lives, some individuals develop more extrovert traits than others. For the most part extrovert traits are desirable but some can be annoying. Introvert persons tend to be more intelligent, more imaginative and more creative than the extroverts. On the other hand extroverts tend to provide more leadership and group action than introverts. You will do well to study the many traits of extroversion and introversion listed above and to decide which of these traits you wish to develop for yourself.

The dominant person is not the one who makes the most noise; he's the one who gets his way by persuasion, expertise or by acclaim of his fellows. He's likely to be as persistent as a dental drill, for he knows what he wants.

The submissive individual shows such characteristic traits as unquestioned obedience, subservience, resignation, humility, indecisiveness, and a need for strong leadership.

Many, but not all, extroverts are dominant. Many, but not all, introverts are submissive.

Few persons exhibit their prevailing traits in *all* situations, nor at all times. Extremes of extroversion, introversion, dominance, or submissiveness border on neuroticism. A balanced executive can call upon useful attributes of any one of the four as necessity indicates.

People, like coins, tarnish when not in circulation. You can develop desirable social traits by joining, and taking an active part in various groups. Moreover—let's face it—in the corporate bureaucracy, whom you know can be as important as what you know.

Emotional maturity

Studies of successes and failures among managers have repeatedly shown conclusively that social development is a must. Emotional maturity and leadership are outstanding traits.

Emotional maturity is a combination of many positive traits discussed in this chapter. The emotionally mature manager listens carefully, weighs facts before deciding, uses tact in criticizing, coaches subordinates, makes prompt decisions, insists on adherence to rules, is impartial in administering discipline, and gives support to his subordinates. He is patient, persistent, tolerant, forgiving, and willing to compromise. He plans his activities and pursues them vigorously.

By contrast the immature manager avoids issues, has a "short fuse," passes the buck, boasts, puts on a tough front, or may be timid or jealous or sarcastic. He may indulge in apple polishing, and suffer feelings of persecution or of guilt. He is likely to have headaches and stomach disorders, be jittery, or go to excess in alcoholism.

Emotional maturity is desirable in a leader. Typically he has a vision or goal, or asks his subordinates to participate in formulating the goal. He knows how the goal can be achieved and is always prepared to help subordinates in achieving it. When problems arise he makes prompt decisions, to clear the path for further action. He coordinates the activities of subordinates, may criticize results but never intentions, gives praise when due. Followers have a benign emotional experience working under the direction of a strong leader, who has a driving need for achievement.

In the past some strong leaders have been emotionally immature. They have ridden roughshod over their subordinates. Some have torn themselves asunder emotionally. Sociologists point out that this type of leadership is fast disappearing from both industry and government.

Most leaders are possessors of power, and mankind's experience shows that frequently power corrupts. Hence you as a manager, in exercising the power entrusted to you, must be careful that you use it in the direction of the common good, and not for selfish aims. If you exercise power wisely you may ultimately tower above your fellows like a giant redwood in a forest of pines.

Abilities

The third factor of success deals with abilities—physical, mental, vocational, and social. These four words open up a large area of possible development.

Your health can be defined as that level of living at which your normal activities are carried on at maximum vigor. This condition is radiant, exhilarating. An ancient axiom says that "a hale cobbler is better than a sick king," and we all know that no matter how much money one has, if he cannot enjoy health, he cannot enjoy life. I have no intention here of sermonizing on this general subject, because you have already been barraged with literature and advice on rules of healthful living: diet, personal hygiene, exercise, fresh air, proper sunshine, avoidance of fatigue, smoking, alcoholic excesses, and overweight.

Psychosomatic medicine tells us also that avoidance of emotional stress is one of the most important contributors to health. Such stress stimulates ductless glands to produce hormones, chemical stimulants that in turn cause changes in body functioning. Dr. Hans Selye has probably done more research on the stress syndrome than any other person. He says that it evolves through three stages:

1. The alarm reaction, when a physical blow to the body, an infection, or an awareness of danger (whether real or fancied), causes the ductless glands to secrete hormones de-

signed to resist the threat. There is a feeling of disequilibrium in bodily functions.

2. The stage of resistance, when the fighting hormones offset the effects of the blow, or the infection, which has attacked the body; however if the threat is a self-induced and continuing emotional state (such as hate, fear, or guilt), the power of resistance to it becomes depleted, opening up the third stage.

3. The stage of exhaustion. This state, long continued, can convert functional disorders such as indigestion or nervousness into organic disturbances such as ulcers, high blood pressure, heart trouble or kidney disease. The body can overcome trauma or infection much better than it can withstand prolonged anxiety, worry or other negative emotions. Some doctors say the best way to handle emotion is by keeping *in* motion, for activity is more helpful than introspection, physical exhaustion sweeter than self-indulgence.

The negative emotions are mostly manifestations of hate, fear and guilt, which I term the "unholy trinity." They give rise to worry—a thin stream of acid trickling through the mind, cutting a deep channel into which all other thoughts are drained.

Efficient environment is conducive to health and energy. Proper lighting speeds up your reading rate and avoids eye strain. The air you breathe has a comfort zone of heat related to humidity and should be free of dust, odors, or other irritants. Shun unhappy, carping, bickering people. Avoid noise and other distractions. If you were to ask me the quickest, although not the most important, way to increase your personal effectiveness I would reply, "Make your environment peaceful and efficient." Just as the ecologist is aware of the importance of environment to the human race, so too should you control the immediate surroundings under which you work and live.

The second kind of important ability is mental development. Poincaré, a distinguished French mathematician, once declared, "Chance favors the prepared mind." It will pay you to sacrifice some present gratification for your future gain. You need to get information, and practice skills of immediate use in your present job. This in turn motivates you to acquire more, and hence do a better job, ultimately providing a foundation for a higher job. Realize that information is static, your thinking is dynamic. However, the occasional torrent of energy that spurts from a turbulent mind is no match for that which streams steadily from an organized mind.

There are devices that can help your memory, such as the calendar on your desk, or a tickler file. Three useful laws of memory are to concentrate on the thing to be remembered, associate it with things which you already know, and repeat it until it is well imbedded in memory. These laws are especially useful in trying to remember the names of people, dates, or vital information.

If mathematics is important in your work or your future, take a course or study a book on statistics, accounting, finance, graphics or whatever subject is pertinent to your success.

Words are messengers of your feelings; they convey more than their dictionary meanings. Hence take care in your word selection. A harsh word, unspoken, leaves you still its master; once spoken, you become its slave. Bitter words have a longer life than kind words. Hence learn to use soft words in hard arguments. Avoid words beyond the comprehension of your listener. If you can't say it simply, you probably haven't thought it through. Learn to use power words—ordinary ideas with dynamite attached; they trigger action as well as transmit information.

Check and double check your reasoning, an ability that distinguishes man from animals. Cool logic is needed in solving perplexing situations, in making difficult choices, in questioning long-accepted ideas or in deliberately reaching for new conclusions. If you follow this path you will amass applicable information and mull over it, pro and con. Finally you will reach that illumined moment when, with a leap of thought, the right answer appears in sharp focus.

Most individuals accept statements, or the existing status, without challenge. Future-oriented leaders question whether what they hear or see is true now, and whether it will continue to be true a year or a decade from now. Sound reasoning normally follows the following five steps: (1) definition of the problem; (2) gathering of pertinent evidence, both subjective and objective; (3) formulation of tentative conclusion; (4) testing of this conclusion under other conditions; and (5) acceptance or rejection of the conclusion.

Conceptual skill is one of the highest traits of innovators and leaders. A quotation from the Bible says that, "Where there is no vision the people perish." Applied to a business, it means that the business either fails, or fails to grow. Imagination is the stuff of which dreams are made. Once your dreams become clear to you, move toward them with confidence, but for your dreams to come true, you must first wake up!

A third grouping of abilities deals with your own job. Most of the chapters of this book have considered things that can contribute to the present and future success of the managerial aspects of your job. The technical aspects will of course be peculiar to the kind of work done and will relate to the needed information and skill. I suggest that you list additional information and skills you need to acquire for outstanding performance of your present assignment, or as preparation for an already identified higher job.

Interests

The fourth element of your ability to develop requires that you have a clear understanding of your own interests and motivations. To gauge your interests, list the ten things in your life (school subjects, topics, activities) that have given you the greatest satisfaction, and the ten which proved most unsatisfying. You may discover that you are strongly interested in working with people or with ideational concepts, mathematics, mechanical objects, outdoor work, music, art, literature, teaching, social service, clerical work, etc.

Knowing your strong satisfiers and dissatisfiers can help you in setting future career goals. These can be short term goals such as a year or two from now. If you prove able to establish a long time goal with certainty, you are in a better position to set sub-goals. How you envision your future can be a strong determinant, or a deterrent, to your motivation to achieve position, honor, wealth, security, health, happiness, creativity or whatever you consider to be worthwhile in your future. If you achieve good health, within you are hidden dynamos of energy merely waiting for you to flick the switch on. However, history tells us that there have been some individuals with great physical impairments, or with constant pain, who nevertheless have been motivated to high achievement.

Age should be no barrier. Do not excuse yourself by saying, "I am too old." A study was made of 400 noted men over the last few centuries and from many lines of activity. Their greatest work or achievements were listed and dated. The ages between 60 and 70 gave birth to 35 percent of the world's greatest achievements; between 70 and 80, 23 percent; and in the years after 80, 6 percent. In other words, 64 percent of the great accomplishments of the world have been brought about by men who have passed their 60th birthday. These figures prove conclusively that the period of the greatest achievement in a man's life comes not in his youth but in the years of maturity.

In American industry the typical top corporate executive is 53 years old, earns between salary and bonus, $100,000 or more, has had some college training, has been in his job as president five years or less and as a background has had general administrative experience or marketing. He endures a work week of 50 to 60 hours and carries enormous responsibility for the decisions he makes and the people he selects. His reward is not just money, title or honor but is also the ecstasy of winning.

Conserve your time

An important aspect of success in your job and in fact in your entire life is your use of time. Most people believe they could have been more successful if they had only had more time. However, they have just as much as anybody else, for time is the only currency that cannot be counterfeited. One problem of your time is how to keep others from using it up, because those who have time to spare usually want to spend it with someone who doesn't.

In your job the principal time wasters are likely to be (1) failure to organize work and correspondence, causing you to waste time looking for needed items; (2) interruptions by telephone or by people "dropping in"; (3) poorly conducted meetings; (4) indecision through inadequate information; (5) doing detail work that should be done by others; (6) prolonged lunch periods or personal business; and (7) disinterest.

You can analyze how you spend your time in five days of a typical week by listing the various things that you do, such as studying correspondence, clerical work, dictation, answering the telephone, interviewing callers, discussions with a superior, supervising employees, conducting a meeting, driving a car, eating lunch, etc. At the end of the five days estimate the amount of time you have spent on each of these activities and then consider which activities in the future you should stress, which you should minimize, and which you should do away with entirely.

Some managerial jobs require the absorption of many reports or correspondence. In this situation, teach your subordinates to process papers before they come to your desk and call your attention only to those which are unusual, which deviate from normal or which require your personal handling. This is applying the exception principle to your job.

Present managers tend to do things learned from a previous generations of managers—a twenty year lag. You need to avoid the handicap of this lag. Set up a carefully conceived plan for your continued intellectual growth. If you cease to invest in your future, you will lose interest! So hitch your wagon to a nearby star, lest you settle for a nearby hitching post. If you don't want much, you'll likely get less.

Strive for emotional maturity in all human relationships. Join and work with groups dedicated to the betterment of mankind. Do something unrelated to the serious business of living: play, social activities, or hobbies. Be creative with your mind or hands. Develop a steadfast faith in a higher power, trust for your fellow men, confidence in yourself.

Accountants calculate a "breakeven point" beyond which added sales yield ever increasing profits. In your business career you, too, have a breakeven point beyond which added effort yields accelerating success. Most people are content to sit on their "status quos"at the break-even point.

Are you?

In bringing this future-oriented book to a close, I can do no better than quote the poet Edwin Markham who said:

> For all your days prepare
> And meet them ever alike.
> When you are the anvil, bear,
> When you are the hammer, strike!

Tomorrow's actions—NOW

Be fearful of the status quo; plan for change in your company and in your personal life.

Use the wide experience of company directors in the operations of your business.

Listen to, and interpret the significance of, insistent voices of employees, consumers, publications, and governments. Substitute fact for opinions.

Repeatedly update your own education through reading, seminars, technical associations, etc.

Improve your environment: home, social, civic, business, etc.

Learn to make effective use of your time; don't let others waste it for you.

Candidly appraise your own weaknesses as to character, temperament, abilities, and interests. Initiate *actions* to strengthen each deficiency.

Understand psychosomatics—how your emotional maturity can aid your health, and vice versa.

Direct your imagination into channels of importance to your future goals.

Look to your personal survival: health, adaptation to change, working habits, emotional maturity, goals, and financial security.

Set your sights on important goals—and keep them there.

Write out a "scenario" of what your management will be doing five years hence—and why.

If your company has a large computer, with high capacity

storage, keep in touch with voice-visual-graphic (VVG) developments which offer dialogue capabilities between executives and the computer.

Plan for changes in organization, personnel, methods, equipment, products, services, etc. Foresee changes that may be imposed upon your company.

Apply high level management practices to product servicing and to service business.

Establish controls to evaluate management performance in both private and public sectors.

Failing to develop incompetent managers, remove or set them aside to make room for others.

In undertaking long range forecasting, compare findings from two or more distinctly different techniques.

Master the use of the critical path method, PERT, and decision trees—with probability estimates.

If you have a boss, help yourself by helping him.

Consider which social institutions have great need for management talent.

Learn the full meaning of such new terms as management information systems (MIS); telecommunication, simulation, systems engineering, and total systems concept.

If your know a foreign language, consider a managerial career that can make use of the ability.

In light of future change suggested in this book, list at least three careers for yourself which should prove ego-satisfying.

Appendix

IN THE COURSE of writing this book, I sent a questionnaire to 60 authorities in various fields asking them to name "jobs that in the next five years will be in considerable demand or that will emerge anew." Some who responded asked that their names, or connections, not be used. The results follow:

Lawrence A. Appley, Chairman of the Board, American Management Associations

1. A new type of manager who might be called "Chief Executive Coordinator." (See also quotation in Chapters 9 and 18.)

2. "A great need for sales managers and top broader marketing executives."

3. Top notch, high caliber labor relations executives.

Guy B. Arthur, Jr., management consultant

1. Chief Executive Officers—statesmen (industry, government, education, churches).

2. Research and Development Managers—with motivation and financial know how.

3. Industrial Engineers—with social sciences and human relations knowledge.

252

4. Managers and Supervisors—who know how to get the best from people (leaders).

Samuel L.H. Burk, personnel consultant and author

1. Human Relations Counsel, Industrial—broad educational and business backgrounds in behavioral sciences.

2. Psychiatrist; adjustment to change—degrees in medicine and psychiatry plus industrial medicine experience.

3. Socio-Economist—ability to foresee, evaluate, and define future socio-economic changes.

4. Organization structure counsel—knowledge of past and present organizational structure practices, ability to adjust or change structures rapidly to suit changes and do optimum job in adjusting people and their job environments to best advantage.

For some time past and at present, the chief personnel officer in a too large majority of companies has been carrying out custodial duties in connection with such subfunctions as recruitment, hiring, placement, training, safety, salary and wage administration, labor relations, employee recreation, and the like. Recognition of the rapidly accelerating rate of change in the socio-economic environment, as it affects people at work and their inter-relationships, has been largely ignored.

James O. Hayes, president, American Management Associations

1. V.P. Logistics—computer expertise and international political knowledge. Several functions will need combining at the top—transportation, purchasing, shipping, stores management, etc. At present these jobs are competing for top management time.

2. V.P. Personnel—behaviorist; negotiator. A new breed is on the way. The demand will be for a behavioral oriented personnel planner and a negotiator (in the broadest sense) to coordinate several functions.

3. Assistant to President—stature, self-effacement, generalist. In various titles this will blossom as president runs out of time. Will require someone who can represent top management to many publics.

Paul W. Kayser, executive vice president, Golightly & Co., International, Inc.

1. Engineers (Petroleum).
2. Financial People—not CPAs but MBAs.
3. Personnel and Industrial Relations—business men with proven track record.
4. Marketing—with a good sales background, not just MBA.
5. Sales Managers—as distinguished from Marketing.

J.W. Miller, Jr., vice president personnel and organization for a large manufacturer

1. Compensation Managers—particular emphasis on employee benefit programs.
2. Organization Development—some background in industrial psychology or related fields.
3. International Employee Relations—directly related experience in overseas operations.

Donald B. Miller, past president of the Society for Advancement of Management

1. Change Agent/Consultant—extensive knowledge of open sociotechnical systems analysis and design.
2. Career Counselor—knowledge of theory and practice in mid-career and beyond counseling.

Dr. Charles A. Myers, director of industrial relations section, M.I.T.

1. Manpower Planner in Personnel Department—knowledge of new projection techniques, relating manpower requirements—from all occupational levels to product and sales forecasts.
2. Organization Development Specialist in personnel department. Drawing on newer behavioral science experience in helping to change organizations of people in directions of organizational goals, with the cooperation and understanding of people involved.
3. Systems Designer for interactive management information systems. Total management information systems are coming and require specialists who can work cooperatively with managers.

4. Computer-based personnel systems specialist. These will develop far beyond present experience, which is mixed.

5. State and local manpower planners. People who are trained to work with new emphasis in national manpower policy, giving states and cities revenue sharing grants for planning their own programs to meet particular needs of those seeking jobs and those requiring people (employers, both private and public).

William C. Patterson, principal, William E. Hill & Co., Inc.

1. Strategic Planning—business concept and implementation.

2. New Venture Management—market and product nurture.

3. Acquisition/Divestiture—business fit; not conglomeration.

4. Multinational Planning—organization for planning.

Walter J. Pedicord, vice president personnel relations, International Business Machines Corporation

1. Energy Coordinator—to monitor impact of energy shortage on personnel related issues; *i.e.*, transportation, layoffs, work day and week, health and safety, etc., and to integrate these into personnel policies and practices.

2. Manager of Human Resources—it is becoming unacceptable to respond to economic and technical dislocation through layoffs. There is increasing need for individuals capable of planning and implementing alternative solutions involving career redirection and training, employee relocation strategies and work load buffer planning.

3. Manager of Retired Employee Relations—the increasing rate of early retirement, inflation, and retiree benefit coverage causes an increasing need for specialists capable of preparing employees for retirement, second career, etc., and integrating the retiree impact into overall personnel policies and practices.

4. Raw Materials Manager—as an outgrowth of increasingly critical material shortages and rapidly changing costs thereof, there should be an increasing need for individuals who can interface with engineering, manufacturing, purchas-

ing, finance, etc., on strategic planning for material substitution.

5. Word Processing Manager—written communication is no longer a narrowly confined secretarial skill but an integrated system involving dictation, copying, automated typing equipment, remote terminals, etc. The management of such complex systems calls for broader skills then heretofore utilized in the secretarial area. It will provide increasing opportunity, particularly for women in management.

Robin Roark, partner, Hay Associates

1. Executive for Reward Management—requires competence to integrate cash compensation programs with non-cash, benefits, near-cash, and perquisites programs so that all are mutually reinforcing.

2. Manager for Retirement Programs—this would be a subordinate job to No. 1. With increased interest on part of federal government in portability of pensions, increasing Social Security benefits, ceilings on executive retirement amounts, there will be increasing demand for an in-depth specialist in this field. Person should be skilled in developing group programs that are maximally responsive to individual needs.

3. Equal Opportunities Manager—the next five years will surely see federal government prosecuting suspected viola tors under the equal pay and equal job opportunity laws. Incumbents would benefit from holding a law degree but should have a thorough command of job evaluation and cash compensation techniques.

4. Executive for Performance Planning and Measurement—there will continue to be increased awareness of the need to relate reward to performance. Skill in business strategy and planning plus management by objectives will be required of people in this position.

Professor William D. Stevens, Department of Marketing, University of South Florida

1. Marketing Systems Analysis—requiring an operations research background, using real time company or industry

data, building and operating simulation models, forecasting or furnishing management with specific recommendations, acting as part of line management instead of staff.

2. Promotion Investigation Research—using very sophisticated social and experimental research to determine the precise effects, attitudinal and action, of advertising or other promotional campaigns, done well enough to stand up as legal evidence. This is similar to the present copy research but done much better.

3. Bank Marketing Research—this position could have in its title any business which has come only recently to espouse fully the marketing concept. Presumably the business would have been doing economic or financial research or even market research from a very limited conceptual framework. A marketing type MBA would greatly enhance and expand their marketing research, especially if he had had recent experience in, for example, the package goods industry, autos, etc.

4. Procurement and Supply Market Research—this will no doubt not be the title but if supply problems and barter solutions persist, more systematic attention will be given to this area in contrast to recent emphasis on demand. It will probably involve the greater use of econometrics and the use of input-output models.

5. Motivation, Perception, Psychographic Research—after some little overstatement and decline this field will probably have its own resurgence as firms have to reshape their product lines so as to use a rifle shot to send limited supplies of limited product lines to well targeted psycho/socio/graphic target markets. Well trained social scientists with business experience will do this work.

Dr. Dale Yoder, Director, Bureau of Business Research, California State University, and *author*

1. Industrial Relations or Personnel Vice President—qualified as a generalist in management with special capability in manpower management.

2. Vice President for corporate ethics and responsibility—capability as a generalist in management.

3. Ombudsman—a high level of credibility and acceptance.

Lewis R. Zeyher, consultant and author

1. Industrial Engineers—predetermined time standards, knowledge and practice in operation research, queing theory, statistical work sampling, simulation (Monte Carlo) technique.

2. Computer Systems Managers.

3. Sophisticated Cost Control Specialists.

4. New breed of plant managers—college trained with practical experience and knowledge of above disciplines.

Director of manpower planning for a large bank

1. Personnel Relations—organization development (OD).

2. Product Management—financial services industry.

3. Marketing Managers—consumer/mass market financing.

Retired vice president of a business research organization

1. Logistical Planning—or; computer programming, information systems, aware of resource scarcities.

2. Human Resource Planning—labor economics, productivity data, sociology, anthropology.

3. Organization Design—industrial engineering plus organizational or behavioral science.

4. Supervisory Training (revival of) to deal with new elements of work force—special background in behavioral science applications, attitude change, etc.

5. Federal Compliance regarding Personnel—knowledge of all federal regulations—to act as chief coordinator of goverment required programs and interfaces with government.

Vice president, administration for a large pharmaceutical company

1. Career Planner—to assist employees in developing a desirable and feasible career path.

2. Human Relations Consultant—to assist line managers in the development or implementation of sound principles of motivation and human relations.

3. Project Specialist—this variation of project management would bring together people who have a special expertise to work on one or more special assignments until they are completed. Individuals would also have a "home" department; *e.g.,* Compensation, Training, etc.

4. Organization Development Coordinator—primary responsibility to bring about change in any organization.

William H. Latham—Executive Director of Society for Advancement of Management

1. V.P., Community Relations—expert in all areas relating to improving corporate image and demonstrating posture of social responsibility—not just profit alone—as "purpose" of organization.

2. V.P., Environment and OSHA—specialist in impact of environmental aspects of operating a business under increasingly tougher controls and requirements, which have become major expense factor—also related to complying with OSHA regulations, which will be stiffened even more as time goes by.

3. V.P., Management Development—continuing need for constant development of management talent to meet ever increasing need for qualified executives who can grapple with tremendous forces of change and obsolescence caused by technological surges in all directions.

Edward A. Tomeski, Professor of Management, Fordham University

1. Management Information Vice President—allocator of information resource (finance, manufacturing, marketing).

2. Management Information Analyst and Designer—knowledge of total organization, environment, and management information systems.

3. Intelligence Specialist—gatherer of sensitive data (the CIA of business community).

Manager, Diebold Research Program

1. Data Base Manager—degree in data processing, operating systems and data base technology.

2. Quality Assurance Manager—Degree in data processing, accounting, knowledge of standards.

3. Manager of Communications—Engineering, voice and data communications devices.

4. ADP Controller-Pricing and Security—same as No. 2 above.

5 Business Systems Analyst/Programming in user func-

tions regarding marketing decentralization—functional area and systems.

Richard R. Crow, Vice President, Personnel, Sherwin Williams Company

1. Behavioral Scientists—organizational development professionals with particular expertise in the area of socio-technical planning; *i.e.,* integrated available know-how of both people systems and technical systems. Also, the ability to work with complex organization structures.

2. Human Resources Managers—ability to apply accounting-type examination of human factors so managers can make better cost-effectiveness decisions about employees.

3. Civic and Community Affairs Managers—ability to coordinate the multitude of interactions that are necessary to serve the social needs of the community in which the business operates.

4. Strategic Planners—ability to analyze and anticipate markets and market shifts so the company can effectively manage necessary strategy changes.

Edward A. Robie, Senior Vice President, the Equitable Life Assurance Society of the United States

1. Management Science Advisor—someone who would apply operations research technique to questions of work organization, corporate strategy, go, no-go decisions, etc.

2. Actuarial work managers—preferably actuaries themselves, but with more management orientation, interests, and skills than is typical today among actuaries who have remained within the "traditional" bounds of professional work in their field.

3. Project Managers—people trained to lead an ad hoc group on a specific, temporary task and then go on to the next with probably different disciplines, organization bases, etc., represented each time.

4. Problem solvers—the other members of the ad hoc task groups referred to in No. 3.

5. Advanced Underwriting Manager—to develop ideas,

concepts, and programs for assigning agents in areas like estate planning, business insurance, pensions, tax analysis, etc. These are fields in which the uses and sales of life insurance are expanding rapidly and in which the growing complexities of tax laws and rulings and court decisions place a particular premium upon real expertise—and the ability to communicate effectively.

6. Marketing Manager—two types: the Marketing Officer for the company of a product line, operating from the home office, and the Agency Manager who is charged with building the sales force and selling the business.

7. Budget and Expense Control Manager—increasing costs and the great difficulty in controlling them in a large company make this a key job that undoubtedly will grow in significance in the next five years and beyond. The need is not for an accountant approach, but for creative and imaginative ideas for managing costs without impairing the over-all effectiveness of the enterprise.

8. Subsidiary management—expertise in the acquisition or creation and supervision of subsidiary operations.

9. Attorneys—to handle defenses in litigation and governmental hearings in the area of consumer attack.

10. Communications Managers—people with expertise in the development and design of communications-based computer systems. The people will need to have a heavy background in the area of teleprocessing telecommunications.

11. Data Base Managers—this position will be a very high level job and the successful candidate will need to have an extensive background in all phases of project development, data security and data base technology. He will also need to be able to interface with multi-user groups and resolve problems between groups efficiently and fairly.

12. Project Managers for large Data Base/Data Communications projects—this position will require extensive background in systems development projects that are very large in scope, normally costing in excess of $1.5 million to develop. The manager must be experienced in data base systems and data communications. He will need the ability to

develop long-range plans for the project and be able to build a competent staff of data processing people to implement the project.

13. Investment Managers—skilled in joint venture negotiation and management.

14. Medical Underwriting—physicians with a background in clinical practice who can be trained in the art and science of medical underwriting.

15. Occupational Physicians—physicians with good clinical training interested in focusing on preventive health care and the special people and environmental problems with which an employee's health service is concerned.

16. Managers of Health Care Delivery Organizations—individuals with managerial and administrative skills, some degree of "entrepreneurial" initiative, ability to work with health professionals and consumers, knowledge of marketing, financial planning, and control.

17. Top Sales Personnel and Account Executives—to provide investment management and employee benefit planning service to major corporations.

18. Managers—with a working understanding of both systems and production operations. With the continued increase in machine applications, there will be even greater need than now to eliminate the separation that usually exists between these two skills.

19. Health Managers—charged with the responsibility of developing corporate ventures in the health field and solving problems related to personal medical care and community health.

Index

Index

265